The Witchcraft Hysteria
of
1692

TABLE OF CONTENTS

PREFACE

"The New Englanders are a people of God settled in those which once were the Devil's territories; and it may be supposed that the Devil was exceedingly disturbed when he perceived such a people accomplishing the promise of old made unto our blessed Jesus–that He should have the utmost parts of the earth for his possession . . . The Devil thus irritated, immediately tried all sorts of methods to overturn this poor Plantation . . . and we have now with horror seen the discovery of such a plot. An Army of Devils is horribly broke in upon Salem which is the center, and, after a sort, the first born of our English settlements, and the Houses of the good People there are filled with doleful shrieks of their Children and Servants, Tormented by Invisible Hands, with Torture altogether Preternatural."

Cotton Mather.

During the witchcraft hysteria that swept through Massachusetts in 1692, more than 400 persons underwent the horror of being accused of practicing witchcraft. Of these, nineteen were hanged, and one old man who refused to enter a plea at his trial was pressed to death as the sheriff and his men piled weights on him to force him to do so. When the hysteria at last abated, approximately 150 persons were in the various jails in Massachusetts, some of whom had already been sentenced to death, while others were still waiting to be tried. By order of the governor in May of 1693, these people were released when their jail and court costs were paid.

At least three women died as a result of the overcrowded and unhealthy conditions to which they were subjected in prison, while the number of those who died at a later time or who suffered mental or emotional breakdowns as a result of their ordeals will probably never be known. Judging by the fact that numbered among the prisoners were a four-year-old girl, several pregnant women, and a large number of elderly people, this last might reasonably be expected to be high.

Although this is admittedly one of the more degrading pages in our history, we cannot pass judgment on those who were involved until we examine both the times in which they lived and the stresses to which they were subjected.

The Massachusetts colonists had been in an almost-constant state of turmoil since they first settled here, and their troubles were greatly increased when Charles II became King of England. Although he allowed the colony to retain its charter, he overturned the ban imposed by the Massachusetts authorities against reading the Episcopal Book of Common Prayer, also decreeing that all freeholders having estates valued at more than 40 pounds sterling and who were of good moral character were from that time allowed to vote in any election in the colony, regardless of which church they chose to attend. In 1664, he appointed four Comissioners to go to the American colonies (Massachusetts, in particular) to study their laws, authorizing them to rescind any they considered to be of a seditious nature or that in any way tended to undermine his authority.

Massachusetts had only recently rid itself of a number of Quakers and Baptists, and when these people learned that the colony would have to grant them complete freedom of worship, several of them returned. To their sorrow, they found that very little had changed, for when the Commissioners left, Massachusetts again began to persecute religious dissenters, whipping, branding, and jailing them, and even punishing those of the Puritans who treated them kindly.

While these persecutions were going on, relations between the colonists and the Indians began to deteriorate, in large part because of the manner in which the colonists treated the Indians. As the Massachusetts population became larger, more lands were needed to properly sustain everyone, and the settlers took more and more lands for themselves, sometimes buying them, but too often stealing what they wanted. The serious lack of communication between these two diverse civilizations inevitably led to the outbreak of the King Philip War in 1675. Although the war lasted only 14 months, ending in August, 1676 with the death of King Philip, a large number of towns were destroyed, tons of needed food were lost, and more than 600 men were killed before peace was restored.

The following year, the Province of Maine was taken away from Massachusetts and given to Sir Ferdinando Gorges, the grandson of the man to whom it had originally been granted. Massachusetts immediately bought it back from Gorges for 1200 pounds sterling. Charles, who wanted to give this vast territory to one of his relatives, offered to buy it back from Massachusetts, but the General Court ignored the offer and even refused to acknowledge that it had been made. Instead, it quickly appointed a Governor to rule the province, and sent him there with an escort of two ships and sixty armed men.

Charles did nothing more about Maine, but he set the wheels in motion that revoked the Massachusetts Charter in 1684, a blow to the Puritan ministers whose political and ecclesiastical powers were drastically abridged by the loss. James II, who succeeded Charles, appointed Joseph Dudley as President of New England. He proved to be only an interim appointee, for he was soon replaced by Sir Edmund Andros.

A group of Episcopalians, knowing that both the King and Andros, himself an Episcopalian, would be sympathetic to them, began to hold services in Boston about this time, conducting them in private homes without an ordained minister. In May of 1686, the Reverend Mr. John Ratcliffe, an Episcopalian clergyman, came to live in Boston, and by the end of that year there were between 300 and 400 people in his congregation. None of the Puritan ministers would share their churches with the Episcopalians, and when Andros arrived to take over the government, he gave them a part of the Town House to use as a temporary church.

Although this was a decided improvement over what they had, neither Andros nor any of the other Episcopalians was completely satisfied. The following May, Andros sent one of his aides to get the key to the South Church. A delegation from the church protested to the Governor, but to no avail, and the Puritans and Episcopalians shared the same meeting house until 1688.

The Episcopalians made several attempts to purchase land on which they could build a church, but the Puritan owners refused to sell them any, arguing that they could not in conscience do anything that would help to establish the very church in the colony that their forefathers had left England to avoid. In spite of this, a small parcel of land was finally purchased, a church was built, and the Episcopalian faith was at last established in New England.

Andros proved to be extremely unpopular with the Puritan leaders in many other ways. One of his first official acts was to appoint one of his men to censor the press. He then levied a series of confiscatory taxes on the people, following this up by ordering that those who wished to do business with his government would have to come to Boston to do so. This worked a hardship on many of the widows and orphans who were waiting for estates to be probated, and he imposed an even greater burden on them by raising probate fees to the highest level since the colony was founded.

To gain control of the entire New England area for himself and his associates, he ruled that the colonists no longer owned the lands they lived on except as tenants at will, declaring that all lands belonged to the Crown from the time the Charter was voided. He stifled most of the opposition to this ruling by abolishing the General Court, thereby giving himself absolute authority over all legal matters in the territories under his jurisdiction.

During his second year in office, New York was added to the territory under his command. At about the same time, he received word that the Maine Indians were preparing to go to war against the English. He immediately conscripted and led an army of 1200 men to Maine to put down the incipient rebellion, but since he set sail during the coldest part of the year, his task force was in trouble almost from the day it set out. He accomplished nothing tangible, while he lost more than 100 men because of the cold and the lack of food. Shortly after he returned to Boston, several Eastern Indians were brought there as hostages. Unwilling to assume the cost of feeding and caring for them, Andros released them, allowing them to join their people in the war against the Maine settlements that erupted the following year.

James issued a "Declaration of Indulgence" in 1687, granting complete freedom of worship to all his subjects. News of this was greeted with as much joy by the Puritans as it was with displeasure by Andros, who had hoped to someday drive the Puritan church out of New England. Having learned that the Boston churches had set aside a Day of Thanksgiving to celebrate the news, Andros posted soldiers at the doors of every church in town to prevent anyone from entering them on the appointed day.

Realizing that they would never again enjoy the autonomy they had had in the past without a charter, the Puritans sent Increase Mather, pastor of the North Church, to England to see if he could persuade the King to grant them a new one. Mather arrived in London on May 25, 1687, and was granted an audience with the King five days later. Although James flattered the Puritan envoy, leading him to believe that he would act favorably on his request, he did nothing more about it. Mather remained in England for five years, returning to Boston on May 14, 1692 with a charter that gave the colonists far less than they had hoped to receive.

When William of Orange successfully asserted his claim to the English throne in 1689, Andros' rule came abruptly to an end. A copy of Prince William's Declaration was brought here that year by John Winslow, this being the first news to reach New England of William's successful coup. Hoping to suppress news of it, Andros ordered Winslow to give him the copy, but when he refused, Andros had him arrested on a charge of carrying a false and treasonous paper into the country. The people reacted to news of Winslow's arrest by arming themselves and attacking the Governor in his mansion, eventually forcing him to surrender his post and his entire government. He and a number of his subordinates were put in jail, then sent to England to be tried. He was set free shortly after he arrived, and in 1692 King William appointed him Governor of Virginia, a post he held until 1698.

In 1690, French raiding parties, augmented by a large number of Indians, attacked and destroyed the settlements at Casco Bay and Salmon Falls in Maine. Angered by stories of atrocities perpetrated by the French and the large number of casualties suffered by the English, Massachusetts raised an army of 500 men to carry the war into Canada. Originally intending to strike Quebec, the authorities were unable to raise money enough to undertake such an ambitious project, and were forced to settle for an attack on Port Royal in Nova Scotia. This force, under the command of Sir William Phips, sailed for Canada in seven ships. At Phips's arrival at Port Royal, the French Governor, holding the fort with only seventy men, surrendered without firing a shot.

The victorious Phips returned to Boston to find the authorities preparing for an all-out assault on Quebec. Although King William had originally promised to supply the money and armaments needed for the expedition if Massachusetts supplied the ships and the men, it was learned, shortly after a force of 2200 men had been conscripted, that William would have to renege on his promise since he was then involved in a war with James II who was trying to regain the throne.

Impatient to achieve the glory of another easy victory, Phips assumed command of this huge expeditionary force. Sailing from Nantasket in a fleet of 36 ships on August 9, he was buffeted about by contrary winds for so long that he did not arrive at his destination until the middle of October. Instead of the weakly-manned, ramshackle fortress he had found at Port Royal, Phips discovered that Quebec was strongly fortified, and capable of withstanding a long, drawnout seige. Undeterred by these facts, Phips sent a peremptory message to the Governor, demanding his unconditional surrender. When this was refused, Phips attacked, sending 1500 men overland while his flotilla sailed into the harbor hoping to batter the fort into submission. The French easily routed the land forces while the heavier guns of the fort just as easily forced the ships to sail out of gunshot range, most of them severely damaged.

Phips began his homeward journey four days later, but he committed so many blunders on the voyage that he lost a number of ships before he arrived in Boston. To make matters worse, when he finally arrived, he found that there was not enough money in the treasury to pay the wages of those who had taken part in the abortive campaign. The authorities had counted on the spoils of war to pay for the entire cost of the operation, and they were forced to meet their obligations to the soldiers by issuing Bills of Credit, the first recorded use of paper money in any of the American colonies. Since the treasury remained almost empty for a number of years, very few of the Bills were ever redeemed.

In 1691, another great fire broke out in Boston which levelled much of the town, while shortly afterward, news was received that an earthquake had destroyed almost 90 percent of Port Royal, Jamaica, with an estimated loss of 2,000 lives. Many of those who were killed were Puritans and had relatives or friends in Massachusetts. Drought and locusts had severely damaged crops in Massachusetts for several years, while outbreaks of smallpox occurred with depressing regularity, and usually with an alarmingly-high mortality rate. Many of the Puritans were certain that most of their troubles were caused by the devil who wished to drive them from New England. When the first accusations were made against the suspected witches, they felt that they could now fight back against the power responsible for their previous sufferings, and this resulted in an outburst of passion that soon turned to hysteria.

It is important to remember that most of the colonists firmly believed in witchcraft and the supernatural, a belief that was not peculiar either to this period in history or this region, since almost all people throughout history have been haunted by a fear of evil spirits. Since most people are afraid of the unknown, those that believed in these beings concluded that they lived in places unlikely to be frequented by humans—places such as deep forests, impenetrable swamps, or abandoned ruins. Strangely enough, this conviction was not restricted to those with little or no education, for even the clergy, the most erudite class during the first 17 centuries of the Christian era, believed in witches as ardently as any of their contemporaries. At least four Popes issued Bulls against witches during the Rennaissance Period, setting standards of belief that are held by many living in these supposedly more enlightened times.

During the 15th, 16th, and 17th centuries, reformers were attempting to correct real or imagined abuses within the various Christian churches, and such was their fanaticism that they created rifts within the entire Christian structure that have not yet healed. In order to contain the influence of those whose religious ideology differed from theirs, most of the European countries condemned as heretics those who practiced any but the religion approved by the state. These dissidents were charged with being under the baleful influence of evil spirits, and a witch hunt of such staggering proportions erupted in Europe during the 16th and 17th centuries that the shame of the Massachusetts colonists is insignificant in comparison.

For example, more than 500 condemned witches were burned to death in Geneva, Switzerland in 1515, and 975 were put to death in Como, Italy in 1524. During two centuries of horror in Germany, 100,000 persons accused of this crime were executed, while the totals in France and Spain were so fantastically high that no attempt at gaining an official tally has ever been successful. During England's "Long Parliament" (1640-1660), 30,000 persons were executed as witches, while 4,000 others lost their lives in Scotland during this period of mass bestiality. To the credit of the Massachusetts colonists, it should be noted that their hysteria abated almost as quickly as it began, in contrast to Europe where witch hunts were still being conducted well into the 18th century.

The figures quoted above are but a fraction of the European total. Unofficial estimates of the total number killed range from one to nine million, the latter figure probably including those who died while waiting to be tried as well as those who were killed as they were being tested to determine their guilt or innocence.

One method employed by the authorities to examine the accused was the water test which attained its greatest vogue during the latter years of the 16th and the early years of the 17th centuries. Its origins are fairly obscure, but it became popular after the publication of a book by Scribonius, a German educator who recommended it as an infallible means of determining the guilt or innocence of a person accused of practicing witchcraft. The book circulated throughout most of Europe, winning adherents in every country. Among these was King James I of England, sometimes referred to as the most learned fool of Europe, who became a firm believer after reading the book. In this test, the accused was crossbound, with his right thumb tied securely to the large toe of his left foot, and his left thumb to that of his right foot, after which he was placed face down in a body of water. He was judged guilty if he managed to stay afloat, and innocent if he sank. Scribonius reasoned that since water was used to baptize those who embraced the Christian faith, God would not allow it to "enfold to its bosom" those who had given their allegiance to the devil.

That the water test was not used in Massachusetts was largely due to Increase Mather who felt it was unreliable because it was recommended and used by members of the Roman Catholic and Episcopal faiths. In common with most of their contemporaries, Increase and his son Cotton firmly believed in the reality of witchcraft, and the latter's influence in the fight against Satan's "horrible plot which threatens to pull down all the churches of New England" was at least as great as that of any other person in the province. He believed that the world was being prepared for the second coming of Jesus Christ who would return only when the "latter-day Israelites" (the Puritans of Massachusetts) had succeeded in driving the devil out of New England.

Margaret and Thomas Jones of Charlestown

Although the Salem cases are fairly well known to almost every student of New England history, there are many who are totally unaware that a large number of other cases preceded the more highly publicized ones of 1692, and that the first execution of a witch took place, not in Massachusetts as might be supposed, but in Hartford, Connecticut, where Alse (Elsie) Young was hanged on May 26, 1647.

The first execution in Massachusetts took place the following year when Margaret Jones of Charlestown was hanged on Boston Common. Arrested in 1647, evidence was introduced at her trial that many of those who came in contact with her malignant touch became deaf, nauseous, or were wracked by violent pains.

In common with so many others who were later charged with the same crime, Margaret was a healer who spent much of her time helping those of her neighbors who were ill, her knowledge of herbal medicines making her as qualified to treat the sick as any of the local physicians. Although she sometimes cured people whose own doctors were unable to help them, she too often nullified the effect of her good works by loudly and publicly scolding those of her patients who sought medical advice from anyone else. Her unusual skills, her abrasive disposition, the fact that many believed she could accurately predict future events, and that she could overhear conversations that took place far beyond the range of those with normal hearing were facts that were introduced with devastating effect at her examination and trial.

After she had been formally accused, a panel of men and women was appointed to search her body for signs of protuberances that might be used to nourish imps or other supernatural beings. Although the committee found one such growth, it had disappeared when she was examined at a later date, although another one was discovered growing nearby.

At her trial, one of her prison guards testified that he once saw her sitting on the floor of her cell with her skirts bunched up above her waist. As he stared in fascination, a small being issued from her body, although a thorough search of her cell failed to produce any further trace of it. A young female servant swore that she also witnessed a similar sight when she was bringing the prisoner some food. It affected her so much that she fainted.

As the evidence mounted against her, the frightened and bewildered woman tried to testify in her own behalf, but, badgered by the judges, the jury, the witnesses, and even by the spectators, she became so confused that she was caught up in a number of lies. Her shrill protestations of innocence only served to convince the jury that she was guilty, and she was hanged on June 15, 1648. That same day, a storm raging in Connecticut damaged a large number of trees and buildings, and it was generally believed that she had caused this disturbance with the aid of the devil, her master.

Her husband Thomas remained at her side throughout most of her trial. Realizing that his loyalty was drawing suspicion to himself, he tried to leave the country on a ship about to sail for the West Indies. He was put ashore when he told the captain that he would be unable to pay for his passage. He had no sooner left the ship than she began to roll to such a degree that it was feared that she would sink. This incident was immediately reported to the County Court that was then in session, and a warrant for his arrest was issued and served. When he was locked up, the ship stopped rolling, proving to the satisfaction of the authorities that he was responsible for the disturbance. Before he could be formally charged with being a witch, he escaped from jail and fled to New York.

While he was still in jail, a number of New Havenites saw the image of a three-masted schooner, under full sail, in the sky above the harbor. The apparition was clearly visible for 15 minutes before it was hidden by a huge billow of either fog or smoke. When this at last cleared, the ship could be seen slowly sinking into the water.

Those who saw this strange sight claimed they recognized her as a ship that had sailed from New Haven two years before, carrying 70 passengers and a cargo worth approximately 5000 pounds sterling. She sank during a storm shortly after she put out to sea, and no survivors were ever reported. The superstitious New Havenites were now certain that its loss was due to the malevolence of Margaret and Thomas Jones.

Since it was comprised of people who held to these and similar beliefs, it is small wonder that the General Court now passed a law ordering that every person suspected of being a witch was to be kept under constant surveillance, and it even seriously considered sending a representative to England to engage one or more professional witch hunters. If this last had been carried out, it is possible that New England might have suffered from a witch hunt proportionately as bad as that which was then taking place in England.

It was no accident that attention in New England would be focused on witches at this particular time, for this was the period when the English Puritans had at last gained control of the English government. A brief study of events in England will help us to better understand those that took place in New England.

When Charles I summoned the "Long Parliament" in 1640, this body passed a law stating that it could not be dissolved without its own consent, then reversed all the tyrannical and illegal acts enacted during the past eleven years while Charles was ruling without a Parliament. It also abolished the High Commission and Star Chamber Courts, the machinery with which Charles and his two chief advisors, the Earl of Strafford and Archbishop Laud, had imprisoned or executed a large number of religious and political dissidents in order to make the King's power absolute. The House of Commons then impeached the Earl of Strafford and Archbishop Laud for high treason. While Strafford was being tried, the House of Commons set aside his impeachment and passed a bill of attainder—in effect, they sentenced him to death without benefit of a trial. Strafford was beheaded in May of 1641, only six months after the Long Parliament was convened. Laud was imprisoned in the Tower of London in February of 1641. After a trial that dragged on until 1644, he was found guilty of subversion, of trying to overthrow the Protestant religion, and of being an enemy of Parliament, for which crimes he was beheaded on January 10, 1645.

Civil war had broken out in England in 1642, and when Charles's army was decisively beaten by Oliver Cromwell at the Battle of Marston Moor in 1644, the Puritans were in complete control of the English government. That same year, Matthew Hopkins, an obscure Puritan lawyer, taking advantage of an ordinance passed in 1641 making witchcraft a felony, began to smoke out the witches in his town, He was so encouraged by his initial success that he assumed the title of "Witchfinder General of England," going from town to town to do the same for a fee of one shilling for each witch he exposed.

Hopkins followed a relatively simple but very effective routine in his investigations, to a great extent copying the tactics of his counterparts in Germany where the "art" of witch hunting originated. He first asked the suspects to confess, and a surprisingly large number of them did so. Those who maintained that they were innocent were then stripped so their bodies could be searched for signs of any growth from which their "familiars" might suckle for nourishment, or for any spot, regardless of how small, that might be insensitive to pain. This last was because it was popularly believed that the devil usually placed his mark on his subjects. Since his touch killed the nerve ends, pins and knives could be stuck into that part of the body without causing any discomfort.

If the suspects passed these preliminary tests, they were bound, cross-legged and naked, and placed in a room where they remained alone for as long as two days and nights without food or water. A small hole was bored in the door of this room to allow their imps to enter. If the suspects still did not confess or show signs of a damning "third teat", they were taken outside, still naked and barefooted, where they were forced to run over a specially-prepared course filled with jagged stones and other sharp objects until they either dropped from exhaustion or confessed. The final test was the one advocated by Scribonius in which the suspect was crossbound and placed face down in a body of water. In view of this thorough examination, it is not too surprising that every person examined by Hopkins was found guilty.

His successes attracted so much attention that special Courts of Oyer and Terminer were set up to try the accused witches he and other witch hunters uncovered throughout the rest of the country. News of their successes soon reached New England where some of the colonists became eager to emulate their English brethren in their fight against the devil and his minions.

Mary Glover of Boston

Several dozen witchcraft cases were tried between 1647 and 1692, each of them having some effect on the outbreak in Salem Village, but the one with the greatest impact and from which the local ministers drew the most analogies was that of Mary Glover of Boston, an Irish immigrant whose imperfect command of English and her volatile temperament were the major causes of her trouble with the law.

She lived near John Goodwin, a fairly prosperous stone mason whose wife had recently given birth to their sixth child. Their oldest son served his father as an apprentice, while the other four, Martha 13, John 11, Mercy 7, and Benjamine 5, were at an age when they required so much more supervision than their mother could possibly give them while saddled with the care of her newborn infant that Goodwin hired Mary Glover's daughter as a part-time housekeeper.

Her first few weeks in her new position passed uneventfully, but during the summer of 1688, Martha accused her of stealing several pieces of linen that had somehow become lost. The domestic denied having done so, but the officious Martha screamed at the young girl until she burst into tears and ran home. When Glover learned of the incident, she stormed over to the Goodwin house to defend her daughter, using such strong language in doing so that Martha suffered a seizure similar to an epilectic fit. John, Mercy, and Benjamin soon followed suit, and the four children remained ill for so long that their worried father sent for a physician to treat them. When he was unable to help them or even identify the disease that afflicted them, he told Goodwin that his children were being troubled by evil spirits.

Cotton Mather came to the house to pray for them, but the children received no benefit from his prayers since the spirits caused them to become deaf whenever he began to speak, forcing the irritated Mather to return to his home in defeat.

Some time later, five ministers—one from Charlestown and four from Boston—conducted a day of prayer at the Goodwin home, hoping to effect in unison what Mather had been unable to accomplish by himself. They were partly successful, for they drove the spirits from Benjamin's body, and he was never bothered by them again.

When the Magistrates learned of the children's experiences, they questioned Goodwin who told them that he suspected that Mary Glover was responsible for their suffering. They called her before them for an examination, beginning it by asking her to repeat the Lord's Prayer. When she was unable to do so correctly, they tried to help her by reciting it with her, but she continued to make so many mistakes that the Magistrates were convinced of her guilt. Asked if she believed in God, she answered it in such a manner that the clerk who was recording the examination refused to write her entire answer on paper. After several more questions, the Magistrates ordered her taken to the jail to await her trial, convinced that she was guilty of the charges against her.

Once Glover was in custody, the children were not tormented as often nor for such long periods of time, leading their parents to hope that the demons would leave them completely. Shortly before Glover's trial, however, the three older children met one of her relatives as they were walking in the street, and they were again afflicted as painfully as before.

At Glover's trial, it was apparent that she could understand very little English and could speak it only with great difficulty, so two men who claimed to know Gaelic were used as interpreters. After a brief consultation with her, they told the Court that she had confessed her guilt, so a constable was sent to search her house for any incriminating evidence that he might find. He quickly returned with several rag dolls. When she was asked what they were, she said that she used them to torment the children, demonstrating how she did so by spitting on her finger and rubbing the saliva on the doll. This caused John Goodwin to go into such wild convulsions that it was sometime before he could be quieted enough to allow the trial to resume. So that there would be no question about her alleged powers, she was asked to repeat her performance, and the child was again affected as before.

Before the Court passed sentence on her, six doctors examined her to determine if she was mentally competent to stand trial. They learned that she was a Roman Catholic, and that she could recite the Lord's Prayer much better in Latin than she could in English, although she admitted that she had stumbled over one particular phrase, even in that language, ever since she was a little girl. She answered all the questions put to her in such a normal manner that the doctors were convinced that she was legally sane, a fact that they reported to the Court.

Mary was found guilty of practicing witchcraft, and sentenced to be hanged on Boston Common. On the day of her execution, she told Cotton Mather that her death would not stop the children's suffering as another witch was still living in the Boston area. Although he begged her to tell him who she was, Glover went to her death without revealing the other witch's identity.

Her prediction was borne out, for Martha, John, and Mercy were now seized with fits at more frequent intervals than at any time in the past. In addition to this, they sometimes barked like dogs, meowed like cats, and constantly complained that the witch was trying to hurt them. Sometimes she drenched them with ice-cold water, tried to push them into the fireplace, or beat them with sticks or cut them with a knife. On several occasions, she carried them through the air to various places they did not recognize, but she brought them home when they would not agree to accept the devil as their master. Although they knew her identity, they were unable to reveal her name for she always struck them mute when they tried to do so.

The children enjoyed a period of relative peace for a short time. At this time, they were afflicted only when their parents reproved them for any reason, or when the words "God" or "Jesus Christ" were mentioned in their presence. During this period, three of the local ministers questioned John, but they were unable to learn anything from him, for the witch plugged his ears so that he did not hear anything they asked.

Cotton Mather brought Martha to live at his house so that he might study her, and she went through a short period during which she suffered no seizures. After a few days, she suddenly cried out, "They have found me," and she was again subjected to periodic torments. She could no longer eat or drink normally, for the witch constricted her throat whenever she tried to do so. She also complained that the witch now made her wear the same chains that had bound Mary Glover during her imprisonment. This tired the young girl so much that she was unable to help with even the lightest household tasks.

Mather encouraged her to read the books in his library while she was resting, but the witch struck her blind whenever the names "God" or "Jesus Christ" appeared on a page she was reading, forcing her to discontinue her studies.

As she sat with the Mather family one evening, she suddenly became rigid, remaining in this state for several minutes. When she was questioned about her seizure, she explained that the witch had carried her through the air to several places, none of which she had recognized. During the entire time, she had ordered Martha to serve the devil, but when the young girl refused, the witch returned her to Mather's house.

On November 27, the five ministers again conducted prayer services at the Goodwin home with all the children in attendance. This marked the end of the children's agony as their periods of torment became less frequent and were not as painful as they had been in the past.

Although Martha was no longer tormented, Mather insisted that she remain at his house until Spring when she at last returned home. He kept her under constant surveillance during her stay, and he later stated that he had learned more about witchcraft by questioning and observing her than he had from all the books he had ever read on the subject. When the hysteria of 1692 broke out, the knowledge he gained during his contact with Martha helped him immeasurably in his campaign against the forces of Satan.

Outbreak at Salem Village

Salem Village, now Danvers, Mass., was set apart from Salem in 1672, but only as a separate parish, for it remained under the political control of the mother town until a much later date. The village was usually referred to as the Farms, and those living there as the Farmers. Most of these people, having

Salem Witch House, Salem, Mass. In this house, the home of Magistrate Jonathan Corwin, were held many of the pre-trial examinations of those accused of witchcraft in 1692. When Major Nathaniel Saltonstall of Haverhill resigned his commission as a Justice on The Court of Oyer and Terminer, Governor Phips selected Jonathan Corwin, a highly-respected member of the Salem Church to replace him. The Witch House, authentically refurbished in the style of that period, is one of the most popular tourist attractions in Massachusetts.

little or no formal education, shared the insecurity so often found in those whose livelihood depends on climatic factors beyond their control and understanding, and since they feared what they were unable to understand, they lived in an almost-constant state of superstitious dread.

Because so many of them were able to scrape only a bare existence from their labors, they were frugal to the point of miserliness, a distasteful fact that was soon discovered by those who served as their ministers. James Bayley and George Burroughs, the first two, resigned their posts for a variety of reasons, the most important being that they were unable to subsist on what the parishioners were willing pay them. They were also caught between two cliques who were trying to control the parish—the rift became so bad that several families rejoined the First Church in Salem in spite of the longer distances they had to travel to services. The ministers and their families, in the uncomfortable position of having to act as mediators in the frequent disagreements that arose between the two factions, were mistrusted by both sides, and were spied on and badgered until they left the village. In fact, Burroughs was arrested in Maine and brought back to Salem on the basis of a warrant charging that he had not paid some of the expenses of his wife's burial, although the Court dropped the charge when Nathaniel Ingersoll, a deacon in the church and the proprietor of the only tavern in the village, produced a receipt proving that Burroughs had long since paid the bill in full.

Deodat Lawson, the next minister to answer the call of the Salem Village parish, served from 1684 until 1688 when he resigned to return to Boston. Searching for a replacement, the Farmers soon found one in the person of Samuel Parris, a 35-year-old former merchant. Parris had attended Harvard College for a time, but dropped out before he completed his studies. He then became engaged, although only in a modest way, in the West Indies trade, living for a short time in Barbados where he purchased two slaves who were to figure prominently in the witchcraft hysteria—John Indian and his wife Tituba.

Although many of those who were involved in the import and export trade in that era became wealthy, Parris's income was so uncertain that he decided to become a minister. In the spring of 1689, after a number of larger churches had refused his services, he submitted his name to Salem Village, naming several conditions that had to be met before he would accept the position, one of them being that he wanted title to the parsonage free of all encumbrances.

Despite the fact that they were unable to find anyone else, the parishioners would not accede to his demands, and the humiliated Parris at last accepted the position on their terms in the late fall. Although his salary was only a modest 66 pounds sterling per year, only two thirds of this was to be paid in cash while the rest of it was to be made up in farm provisions.

When he moved into the parsonage in November, he put the past behind him, and entered into his duties with all the energy and zeal of a newly-won convert. He was singularly lacking in humor, and his home was devoid of anything that might distract its occupants from the seriousness of the Puritan creed.

Besides his wife, his daughter Elizabeth, and his two Indian slaves, he also had his niece Abigail Williams living with him. Since the two Indians performed most of the work in the home, Mrs. Parris was able to spend most of her time making parish calls, while the two girls were responsible for only a few of the lighter household chores.

Events went on at a relatively-normal pace until the winter of 1691-1692. During those long winter afternoons, the nine-year-old Elizabeth and the eleven-year-old Abigail were too often left alone to study religious lessons while the Parrises were occupied elsewhere. Although they had done so dutifully in the past, both soon tired of the tedium of their studies. Looking about for anything that might brighten the dreariness of their everyday lives, the two girls soon found an alluring possibility—Tituba.

Each afternoon, the two would sit in the kitchen while the West Indian regaled them with stories of her childhood in Barbados where she had become proficient in the arts of voodoo and hypnotism. Needless to say, the girls were enchanted by Tituba's stories that pictured a childhood so romantically different from their own.

Unable to keep their secret to themselves, they invited Ann Putnam, Jr., the twelve-year-old daughter of the parish clerk, to join them, and the group was in time enlarged by the addition of three servant girls and four other young ladies, all of them under twenty years of age. On occasion, several married women, one of them Ann's mother, also attended the exciting afternoon get-togethers, in spite of the fact that much of the conversation centered on subjects, such as voodoo, which were strictly forbidden in the Puritan community.

Tituba's stories were told with such realism that the two younger girls were quite visibly affected by them. Shadows in the corners of familiar rooms were turned into grotesque apparitions by their imaginations, and what had started out as a harmless pastime was now responsible for a series of horrifying nightmares. There is reason to believe that Tituba might have demonstrated her knowledge of hypnotism to the group, using the younger girls as subjects, for Elizabeth soon developed a disturbing habit of gazing into space for long periods as though in a post-hypnotic trance. This mood would invariably be followed by seizures similar to the ones that had affected the Goodwin children four years before. While in the throes of these seizures, she would crawl about the room on her hands and knees emitting hoarse, choking sounds. Abigail was soon similarly affected, and their strange actions so alarmed Parris that he asked Dr. Griggs, the local physician, to look at them.

Griggs dosed the girls with several medicines, none of which had any effect, for the girls continued to creep about uttering strange unintelligible sounds, and complaining that sharp objects were being pressed into their flesh. When he was unable to effect a cure, Griggs solemnly told Parris that the girls were "under the evil hand," meaning that a witch or witches had cast them under a spell, an ominous diagnosis that was soon known by everyone in the village.

The distraught Parris asked the ministers of all the neighboring towns to come to Salem Village and join him in a day of fasting and prayer to drive the evil spirits away. Several accepted the invitation, but after the day was over with no improvement in the girls' condition, they concurred with the finding of the doctor. When they asked the two girls to name those who had afflicted them, Abigail and Elizabeth remained mute, refusing to speak out against anyone.

Tituba was as concerned about the girls as Parris. When a local woman suggested that she could drive the evil spirits away by baking a cake in which she had added some of the girls' urine and feeding it to the Parris dog, she did so. Parris went into a towering rage when he learned of the experiment. He whipped Tituba for casting spells in a Christian household, and preached a sermon the following Sunday in which he accused both women of being far more interested in the arts of Black Magic than they were in the tenets of Christianity.

Still enraged, he returned to the girls, questioning them with renewed vigor. Hoping to jog their memories, he named several people who might be responsible for their suffering. When he mentioned Tituba's name, Elizabeth repeated her name, and Parris accepted this as an accusation. He continued to badger the two girls until Abigail repeated the names of Sarah Good and Sarah Osborne, two of the least popular women in the community.

Parris immediately told the local Magistrates what he had learned, and on February 29 the three women were served with warrants ordering them to appear for questioning at Ingersoll's Tavern at 10 A.M. the following day. Jonathan Corwin and John Hathorne, the two Salem Magistrates who were to examine them, found such a large crowd gathered to witness the proceedings that they transferred the examination to the meeting house which could more easily accommodate all of them.

Sarah Good, an old-looking woman in her early forties, was married to William Good, a laborer whose marginal income had to be supplemented with charity in order for his family to subsist. When he was hired to do odd jobs, he invariably brought his wife with him, and her eccentric behavior in these households was introduced as evidence against her by fifteen of his former employers. Some of these people accused her of destroying their cattle by bewitching them, and blamed her for every misfortune they had suffered since they first knew her. Some even claimed that she manufactured dolls to torment anyone with whom she was displeased, but a thorough search of her home failed to produce any of these crude images.

With Ezekial Cheevers taking notes, the Magistrates began their questioning of Good. She denied that she was familiar with any evil spirits, that she had made a contract with the devil, had tormented the children, or had employed anyone to do so for her. Asked why she had once left the Parris house muttering to herself, she explained that she was merely thanking him for a gift he had given her daughter. When Hathorne asked her why she muttered to herself so often in public, she answered that she did this when she repeated sections of the Psalms she had committed to memory. Ordered to repeat one of these Psalms by the sceptical Hathorne, she did so without an error.

Asked what God she worshipped, she replied that it was He who had made heaven and earth. She did not pronounce the word "God" while she was on the stand, a fact that was noticed by many of the spectators and duly recorded by Cheevers, who added that her answers were given in "wicked and spiteful ways, reflecting and retorting against the authority with base and abusive words."

Since she denied having tormented the children, she was asked who had, and she answered that it was Sarah Osborne. Her husband, from whom she had been separated for several months, told the Magistrates that she had always been an enemy of God, and that in late years she had treated him so abominably that he was convinced that she was a witch.

Tituba, who was questioned next, at first denied that she had ever seen the devil or that she knew who was responsible for tormenting the girls. When the question was put to her a second time, however, she admitted that she was a witch and that she had seen Sarah Osborne, Sarah Good, and two other women, neither of whom she could identify, tormenting them. She also admitted that she had seen a tall man, a native of Boston whose identity was unknown to her, molesting them at other times. This man was usually accompanied by a large group of witches, all of whom badgered her constantly to torment the children. Whenever she refused, they beat her with sticks until she could no longer stand the pain. In spite of this treatment, she asserted that she had tormented the children on only one occasion, swearing that she would never do so again even though the devil commanded her. In fact, she stated that she once refused to obey the devil when he commanded her to kill the children. She admitted that she had seen him on four different occasions, each time in a different guise—once as a hog, once as a dog, and twice in human form. When she told him that she would no longer serve him, he threatened to punish her more severely than she had ever been punished before. She remained adamant, however, and he tried to win her allegiance by tempting her with an assortment of attractive articles, among which were yellow birds and brightly-colored ribbons. When she still refused, he first turned into a red rat and then into a black rat, commanding her to serve him after each transformation.

Tituba further testified that shortly before the examination began, he brought Elizabeth Hubbard to her and forced her to pinch the young girl. On the previous evening, he brought her to the Thomas Putnam house where he ordered her to cut Ann, Jr.'s head off with a knife. When she refused, he jabbed the point into various parts of the girl's body, although he was careful not to draw any blood. One of the spectators interrupted her testimony to state that while he was at the Putnam house the previous evening, Ann, Jr. complained that a band of witches had threatened to cut her head off with a large knife.

In response to a query about how she and the other witches travelled, she explained that they rode through the air on sticks, although they flew so fast that she was unable to say whether they went through or over natural obstacles such as trees and mountains.

Asked why she had never told her master about her association with the witches, she said that they threatened to cut her head off if she told anyone. When she was asked if her sister-witches had any attendants or familiars, she replied that Good had a yellow bird, while Osborne had a creature with two legs, two wings, and a woman's head. This last-named creature sometimes disappeared into Osborne's body, while at other times it assumed her identity. Tituba claimed that she had also seen another creature with Osborne. This one walked on two legs like a human, but it had long, coarse hair growing from every part of its body. She further stated that Osborne and Good had tormented Jonathan Corwin's son the previous night, after which they unleashed a wolf to frighten Elizabeth Hubbard.

At several points her testimony was interrupted by the afflicted girls who screamed so loudly that the proceedings had to be stopped until they again became quiet. When she was first asked who was tormenting the girls, she answered that it was Sarah Good, but when the girls began to scream again, she told the Court that she could no longer see who was bothering them since the witches had taken away her spectral vision.

Sarah Osborne was examined next. She immediately denied having any knowledge of spirits, witches, devils, or other supernatural beings, then stated that she had not seen Sarah Good for two years and could not help it if the devil travelled about in her likeness. Some of the girls testified that she had hurt them in the past, but Osborne retorted that it was more likely that she was bewitched than that she was a witch, explaining that she had only recently had a dream in which a dark-skinned Indian appeared before her. He disappeared after pinching her on various parts of her body. On further questioning, she admitted that a voice had once commanded her to stop attending church services, but she claimed that she had defied it by going to meeting the very next Sunday. When Hathorne wanted to know why she had not attended meeting during the past fourteen months, she explained that she had been extremely ill during this period, adding that she would be in bed at this very moment if the constables had not arrested her.

The three women were examined again the following day, then Sarah Good and Tituba were examined on March 5. Throughout each examination, Tituba insisted that Sarah Good and Sarah Osborne were witches, and the three were at last sent to jail to await trial. While they were in jail, Tituba was examined again, this time in her cell, and she again confessed that she had once been a witch. She told her examiners that she was now one of the afflicted persons, for the devil was constantly tormenting her in order to regain her allegiance, showing them marks the devil had put on various parts of her body. This, plus the fact that she answered the questions put to her exactly as she had during the previous examinations, convinced the Magistrates that she was telling the truth.

Sarah Osborne was much sicker than she or anyone else realized, for she died in jail on May 10, insisting to the end that she was innocent of the charges against her. Sarah Good, who was in an advanced state of pregnancy, had her child while she was in prison, but because of the unsanitary conditions to which he was exposed and the haphazard care given him, he died shortly after he was born.

Other girls began to complain that they were afflicted by the witches, naming not only Good and Osborne as their tormentors, but also several others who were soon arrested. The Magistrates, ministers, clerks, and everyone else concerned with the examinations conscientiously tried to learn all they could about the history of witchcraft and the manner in which the authorities in England had handled the problem during Cromwell's reign. As they read far into the night, the clamor of the afflicted girls became louder as they began to accuse more and more people of being involved with the devil.

Deodat Lawson's Experiences in Salem Village

The Reverend Mr. Deodat Lawson, who had served the Salem Village church as its minister from 1684 to 1688, was living in Boston when the hysteria erupted. Learning that the afflicted girls had accused a suspected witch of causing the deaths of his wife and daughter, he went to the village hoping to learn more.

Arriving there on March 19, he first engaged a room at Ingersoll's Tavern which was almost directly across the street from the parish house, then went to the taproom where he chatted for some time with Mary Walcott, one of the afflicted girls. As Mary was leaving, she stopped at the door and cried out that one of the witches had bitten her on the wrist. Examining her wrist by the light of a candle, he clearly saw the impression left by a set of teeth.

Later that evening, he went across the street with Deacon and Mrs. Ingersoll to pay his respects to Parris. During his visit, Abigail Williams was tormented by the spectre of Rebecca Nurse, a local woman who was a member of the First Church of Salem. The spectre, unseen by everyone in the room but Abigail, pushed her back and forth across the room with such force that she might have been seriously hurt but for Mrs. Ingersoll, who held the young girl in her arms.

The spectre finally succeeded in tearing Abigail away from her protector, then tried to force her to sign a book she held out to her. Abigail shouted that she would not sign it for she believed that it was the devil's book, then ran to the fireplace where she pulled blazing sticks out of the fire and threw them about the room. While the older people picked them up to prevent the house from catching fire, she ran to the rear of the fireplace as though she intended to climb up the chimney. After she was at last quieted, Parris told his visitors that she had narrowly escaped injury from burns on a number of other occasions when she was being tormented by the witches.

Lawson officiated at church services the next day, totally unprepared for what took place. Many of the afflicted girls were present, most of them going into witch-induced fits throughout almost the entire service. After the congregation had finished singing a Psalm, Abigail Williams rose and ordered Lawson to name his text. Told what it was, she complained that it was a very long one. He had been speaking for a short time when he was interrupted by another of the afflicted girls who said that he had talked long enough.

During the afternoon service, Abigail again interrupted him while he was speaking, while Ann Putnam, Jr. cried out that a yellow bird was sitting on the pin on which Lawson's hat was hung, a strong indication that the afflicted girls were seriously considering crying out aginst him. Later in the afternoon, Abigail cried out, "Look where Goody Cory sits on the beam suckling her yellow bird betwixt her fingers." After this outburst, the services were concluded without further incident.

The next day, Lawson attended the examination of Martha Cory, and on Wednesday he visited the Thomas Putnams, hoping to ask Ann, Sr., one of the afflicted persons, some questions. When he arrived, Ann was in bed recovering from a seizure she had had a short time before he came. She and her husband both begged him to pray with them until she was free of her afflictions, even though the spectre had told Ann that it would not allow him to do so. Ann was so quiet while he was praying that he thought that she had fallen asleep, yet, when her husband went to her, he found that she was as rigid as a board. He picked her up, hoping to cuddle her on his lap, but her legs were locked so stiffly that he had trouble bending them. After he seated her on his lap, her arms and legs began to flail about so violently that Thomas was forced to exert all his strength to hold her. While all this was taking place, she kept up a conversation with the apparition.

At one point she cried out, "Goodwife Nurse. Be gone! Be gone! Are you not ashamed, a woman of your profession (a professed Christian) to afflict a poor creature so? What hurt did I ever do you in my life? You have but two years to live, and then the devil will torment your soul. For this your name has been blotted out of God's Book, and it shall not be put in God's Book, again. Be gone, for shame, are you not afraid of that which is coming upon you? I know! I know what will make you afraid: the wrath of an angry God. I am sure that will make you afraid. Be gone. Do not torment me. I know what you would have, but it is out of your reach. It is clothed with the white robes of Christ's righteousness."

Continuing her conversation with Rebecca's apparition, she argued about a particular text in the Bible, all the while keeping her eyes tightly closed. Ann shouted that there was such a text, and that she was going to say it aloud, forcing the apparition to leave since she was certain that those who had signed the devil's book could not remain in the same room in which this text was being read. When she made this threat, she was again taken by a violent seizure in the course of which her mouth was drawn violently to one side. Seizing her opportunity when the spectre had relaxed its hold on her, she cried out, "It's the third chapter of Revelations." Lawson quickly opened the Bible to that chapter, and when he began to read aloud, Ann's seizures were ended.

Rebecca Nurse was arrested the following day. From the time of her arrest until April 5, the day Lawson returned to Boston, Ann Putnam, Sr. suffered no more seizures.

Massachusetts Receives a New Charter

On May 14, 1692, after an absence of five years, Increase Mather returned to Boston with Sir William Phips, the newly-appointed Governor of Massachusetts, and a new charter. Although Mather had been unsuccessful in his efforts to convince King William to grant the Massachusetts colonists the same liberties they had enjoyed under the old charter—the Governor and Deputy Governor were now appointed by the King instead of being elected by the people, and all freeholders of estates valued in excess of forty pounds were eligible to vote in all elections in the colony, regardless of which church they chose to attend—he did convince him to appoint Sir William Phips and William Stoughton, both ardent Puritans, as Governor and Deputy Governor, respectively.

When the two men arrived, the colony was involved in a war with the Indians in Maine and more than fifty accused witches were already in the various Massachusetts jails waiting to be tried. Since Phips had very little training in any aspect of the law and none in theology, he was unprepared for the problems regarding the witches that needed attention. At Increase Mather's suggestion, he appointed a committee of twelve ministers to set up rules governing the trials. On May 25, he commissioned a special Court of Oyer and Terminer to try the witchcraft cases, and on May 27, he appointed seven Justices to serve on the Court, designating Deputy Governor Stoughton as its Chief Justice.

The ministers went to work almost immediately. Convinced that the devil could assume the body and features of any person, regardless of how pious and innocent of wrongdoing that person might be, they recommended that spectral evidence—instances in which the spectre of a person was seen performing acts of witchcraft while the person was elsewhere and unaware of what was taking place—be disallowed in the coming court cases. Once they had completed their task, they assigned Cotton Mather the responsibility of writing the final draft. While he followed their recommendations faithfully, he very skillfully and effectively nullified the one pertaining to spectral evidence by adding a postscript of his own in which he praised the authorities and the members of the Court for their diligence in detecting and prosecuting the witches to this date. He urged them to continue their good works in all the subsequent cases, making certain that they were guided by the laws of God and the English statutes at all times. By the time the paper was completed and given to Chief Justice Stoughton, on June 15, Bridget Bishop had already been tried, condemned, and executed, all on the basis of spectral evidence. Since none of the Salem Magistrates or the Justices on the Court had any formal legal training, they assumed that they were to continue on in the same manner, and every person found guilty of practicing witchcraft during the next three months was judged and executed on the same type of evidence.

The Case of Bridget Bishop

On April 19, warrants were served on Giles Cory, Mary Warren, and Bridget Bishop, the last-named being the person to whom must go the dubious distinction of being the first person to be tried by the Court of Oyer and Terminer and the first of the nineteen unfortunates to be hanged.

After Bridget was arrested, she was examined by John Hathorne and Jonathan Corwin, who first ordered a panel of nine women and a doctor to search her body for evidence of any growth from which imps or devils might suckle. After a thorough probe, they found one growing close to her pubic area. A pin passed through it produced no visible signs of discomfort. Three hours later when Hathorne and Corwin had finished questioning her, she was again searched by the panel who discovered that the first growth had disappeared but that another was growing nearby.

Bridget was probably the most unpopular of all those who had been arrested to this time. This was partly due to the fact that although she was not a beautiful woman most men were attracted to her because of her flair for showing off her voluptuous body to good advantage with the aid of brightly-colored clothing, in marked contrast to the sombre garb affected by most of the local women.

She owned a tavern near the Salem-Beverly line that was a popular hangout for many of the younger men of both communities, and her neighbors were quick to notice whenever she allowed a select few of her customers to remain in the tavern when those with more normal sleeping habits had already retired for the night.

Goodwife Christian Trask was one of these. She was of an unstable temperament, and her obsessive study of the Book of Revelations, from which she hoped to learn the mysteries of the future, only tended to aggravate her mental condition. Probably egged on by some of the other neighborhood women, she forced her way into the tavern one night when it was filled with young men shouting encouragement to a group playing a harmless game of shuffleboard. She gathered up the game pieces, threw them into the fire, angrily ordered everyone to leave, then shrilly lectured Bridget for some time. The following Sunday, as Bridget was about to receive the Sacrament, Trask rose from her seat to say that Bridget was unworthy of the honor.

She later apologized to Bridget, who not only forgave her but even tried to become her friend. In spite of this, Trask's mental condition deteriorated to such an extent that she became a disturbing factor at church services, interrupting the minister and distracting the congregation by her shouts and antics. Although aware of her conduct, she was unable to control it, and her outbursts were invariably followed by periods of depression brought on by a deep-seated feeling of shame and guilt. During one of these periods, she committed suicide by slashing her wrists with a pair of scissors. The Reverend Mr. John Hale, minister of the Beverly church, testified at Bridget's trial that it was his opinion that Trask could not have killed herself with such a small pair of scissors without supernatural aid, hinting broadly that this aid came from Bridget who he also blamed for her mental condition.

Testimony was also introduced that during a visit to the home of Samuel Gray, Bridget spent some time looking down at his daughter who was asleep in her crib. When the baby became ill and died two weeks later, the distraught father swore that Bridget had bewitched the child.

William Stacy testified that Bridget was one of the few people brave enough to visit him when he had smallpox in 1678. When he was well again, she hired him to do some odd jobs for her. Several minutes after he had put the money she paid him in his pocket, he was unable to find it, the first in a weird series of events in which he and she were involved.

He once stopped his wagon to speak with her. After he started up again, one of his wheels became stuck in a rut, forcing him to get help from some passersby to free the wheel. When he later searched for the rut, he was unable to find it.

Another time, his horse stopped short when Bridget walked by. Stacey whipped the animal to get it moving forward again, but no matter how much the horse strained, he was unable to move the wagon. Stacey became so angry that he whipped the horse until it lunged forward, snapping the harness so that the wagon rolled backwards down the hill where it finally smashed into a tree. Another time, he tried to lift a bag of grain onto his wagon as Bridget was walking by, but he was unable to budge it. When she was out of sight, he picked the bag up easily.

A short time after this incident, he was awakened at midnight by her apparition that was crouched on his window sill. The entire room was lighted up by the glow that enveloped her. She jumped down from the sill, then hopped about the room with her cloak wrapped tightly about her legs. When she left a few minutes later, the room was again plunged into darkness.

As he was going to his barn at dusk a few days later, he was suddenly hoisted into the air, slammed against a stone wall, dropped back onto the ground, and then rolled down a steep embankment. The next morning, as he was driving his wagon, a wheel fell off as he passed Bridget, causing the wagon to collapse. In 1690, his young daughter became so ill that he called in a doctor to attend to her. In spite of the doctor's care, the young girl died, a fact that Stacey attributed to a spell cast by Bridget.

Other serious charges were brought against her by Samuel Shattuck, a Quaker who operated a tailor shop in Salem. He testified that she once commissioned him to dye several bits of lace which he later sewed onto her dresses. He placed the money she paid him in a purse which he then locked in a heavy wooden box, but when he later opened the box, both the purse and the money were gone.

He added that shortly after his wife and Bridget had a serious argument in 1678, his oldest son was stricken with a disease that left him "stupefied and void of reason." Neither the local doctors nor those he consulted in England could cure the boy, but they were all agreed that he was "under the evil hand of witchcraft," proving to Shattuck that Bridget had used this means to settle her argument with his wife.

John Bly testified that he once bought a sow from Bridget's husband who told him to pay the money to a third person, possibly someone to whom Bishop owed a similar amount. When Bridget learned of this agreement, she became livid with rage, and screamed at him for some time. After her temper cooled, she allowed Bly to take the sow, apparently dismissing the matter from her mind.

When the sow had its next litter, however, it began to act in a strange manner, refusing to eat or to suckle her young. She leaped into the air, and ran about her enclosure, frequently banging her head against the walls of her pen. A neighbor who witnessed these antics advised Bly to destroy the animal as he was certain that she was bewitched.

Some time later, Bridget built a new home and hired Bly to dismantle the cellar wall of her old house. He told the Court that in the course of the work, he and his son found a large number of rag dolls, with pins and hog bristles stuck in them, secreted in recesses in the cellar wall.

John Lowder, a 24-year-old laborer who worked for Bartolomew Gedney whose farm abutted that of Bridget, testified that he had once complained to her that her chickens were causing a great deal of damage to Gedney's garden and orchard, and that she agreed to keep them penned only after a long and violent argument. Several days after the argument, he was awakened by a heavy weight on his chest. Since the room was brightly illuminated by the moon, he saw that it was Bridget sitting on him. She imprisoned his hands and began to choke him, allowing him to breathe just enough to keep him from passing out.

The following Sunday, Lowder stayed away from church services because he felt ill. Although every door in the house was closed, a black pig managed to enter his bedroom. He kicked at the animal, but it dodged away and disappeared. While the unnerved young man lay down to rest, a black creature with the body of a monkey, the feet of a rooster, and the face of a wizened old man flew into the room, alighting only a few feet away from him. The creature told him that he was a messenger from the devil who, aware of Lowder's financial troubles, promised that he would never want for anything during his lifetime if he agreed to be ruled by him. Lowder bravely tried to grab the creature who easily eluded him. Lowder struck at it with a stick, but missed, and the stick hit the ground with such force that it splintered, leaving his arm numb from the shock. When Lowder went outside to look for the creature, it had disappeared, but he saw Bridget walking in her orchard some distance away.

The creature reappeared when Lowder returned to his room. The distraught young man cried out, "The whole armor of God be between me and you," after which it flew out the window, the vibrations from its wings causing a large number of apples to fall off the trees. In taking off, the creature kicked some gravel against Lowder's stomach with such force that he was unable to speak for three days.

Cotton Mather, who wrote a short account of her trial, stated that as she was being brought to the court house from the jail, she "gave a look towards the (meeting) house, and immediately a demon invisibly entering the meeting house tore down a part of it; so that though there were no person to be seen therein, yet the people at the noise rushing in, found a board which was strongly fastened with several nails, transported into another quarter of the house." He further stated that there was so little doubt as to her guilt that "there was little occasion to prove the witchcraft, it being evident and notorious to all beholders." On the basis of this and other similar evidence, she was found guilty by the jury, sentenced to die by the Court, and was hanged at Gallows Hill in Salem on June 10, the first person to be executed during the witchcraft hysteria.

The Case of Rebecca Nurse

Rebecca Towne Nurse of Salem Village, a 71-year-old mother of eight children, was hanged on Gallows Hill on July 19, 1692 along with four other women who had also been found guilty of practicing witchcraft. To this time in the history of the madness, Rebecca must be considered the person least likely to be accused of this crime as she was a deeply-religious woman, respected for her many charitable works, and long considered a pillar of the community.

Although the Nurses were only of moderate means, they owned a 300-acre farm which they had purchased from the Reverend Mr. James Allen, at that time minister of the First Church of Boston. This farm was originally part of Governor John Endicott's estate, the bulk of which was inherited by his son, Dr. Zorobabel Endicott. When his brother John's widow married Allen, Zorobabel gave the couple the 300 acres as a wedding gift, and after she died, Allen sold the entire farm to Francis Nurse, incurring the displeasure of Dr. Endicott by doing so, since he felt that the land should have been returned to him.

The Nurses could not have bought the property except for the fact that their children, seven of whom were married, agreed to work together to pay off the mortgage. They were involved in a landsuit shortly after they assumed possession of the farm, for Endicott claimed that a woodlot joining the two properties belonged to him. Although the court found in favor of the Nurses, Endicott refused to accept its judgment gracefully, and he maintained a coolness toward his unwanted neighbors until the day he died.

During the first weeks of the excitement caused by the accusations against Tituba, Good, and Osborne, Rebecca joined with others in the community in denouncing the actions of the afflicted girls, convinced that the three women were innocent. Once her views were known by the girls, they protected their newly-acquired positions of importance by accusing Rebecca of being one of their tormentors. The Magistrates at first refused to issue a warrant for her arrest, managing even to suppress any news that she had been accused from leaking out for some time. As early as the middle of March, however, rumors began circulating that a highly-respected member of the community would soon be arrested, charged with practicing witchcraft. The warrant was issued on March 23, and she was examined at the meeting house the following day. The witnesses against her were Ann Putnam, Jr. and Abigail Williams, both of whom claimed that she had tortured them because they would not sign the devil's book.

When the examination began, Hathorne first asked the two girls if this was the woman who had hurt them. Abigail answered that it was she, while Ann said that she had beat her that very morning. After she said this, Ann was taken by such violent pains that the examination was stopped until Rebecca's spectre no longer tormented her.

Hathorne then asked Rebecca what she had to answer to the accusations, and she protested her innocence in such a manner that Hathorne spoke to her in a much gentler voice, telling her that he and everyone else in the meeting house respected her so much that they sincerely hoped that she would be able to prove it. Rebecca told him that she had been so ill the past week that she had remained indoors, usually in bed, so that it would have been impossible for her to have harmed the children as they alleged.

The Magistrates and many of the spectators were now so convinced that she was innocent that the case against her might possibly have been dismissed but for the fact that Ann Putnam, Sr. cried out, "Did you not bring the black man with you? Did you not bid me tempt God and die? How often have you ate and drank your own damnation?"

Sensing that the spectators were beginning to have doubts about Rebecca's innocence after this outburst, the afflicted girls again began to howl, screaming that Rebecca's spectre was tormenting them. When Mary Walcott and Elizabeth Hubbard also accused her of hurting them, the examination was resumed.

A number of people were prepared to testify against her. Goodwife Sarah Houlton stated that when her husband's pigs once destroyed part of the Nurse's vegetable garden, Rebecca went to the Houlton home where she upbraided him for allowing them to get loose. A few weeks after this incident, he died unexpectedly, convincing Sarah that Rebecca had put a curse on him.

Henry Kenney asserted that Rebecca cast a spell over him so that he was unable to breathe properly when she was near him, while Edward Putnam testified that he had seen his neice, Ann, during one of the fits which had been induced by Rebecca.

Hathorne recessed the examination so that a panel of women could search Rebecca's body for evidence of witch marks. They reported that they had found several. Although Rebecca complained that these were natural growths that could be found on any older person, the Magistrates refused her request to be examined by another panel.

When it became apparent that Rebecca was too tired to answer any more questions, the Magistrates ordered her taken to the Salem jail where she remained until April 11 when she and five other accused witches were reexamined, this time by Deputy Governor Thomas Danforth, the two Salem Magistrates, and four members of the Governor's Council. Because of the presence of Danforth and the Council members, it should be noted that the hysteria was no longer a strictly local affair, but one that concerned the entire colony. The transcript of these examinations, taken by Samuel Parris, no longer exist, having been either lost or stolen some time in the past. When this tribunal had completed its task, the six defendants were taken to the jail in Boston where they were to be held until they were tried.

Rebecca was tried by the Court of Oyer and Terminer in Salem on June 29. Although a testimonial to her character, signed by twenty citizens of Salem Village, was read to the Court, the Chief Justice ordered her trial to begin.

Ann Putnam, Jr. testified that Rebecca had killed six children, while Sarah Houlton again told the story of her husband's murder. The ranks of the afflicted girls had been swelled by the addition of several older women, one of them being Sarah Bibber, a moderately wealthy young matron. One of Rebecca's daughters complained to the Court that she kept a close watch on Bibber during the proceedings, and had seen her prick herself with a pin, after which she had cried out that the defendant was tormenting her.

When all the evidence had been presented, the jury retired to deliberate, and Thomas Fiske, the foreman, soon returned to the courtroom with a verdict of not guilty. The afflicted girls and some of the spectators made such an outcry when the verdict was read that Chief Justice Stoughton asked Fiske if he had heard the prisoner when Deliverance Hobbs, a confessed witch, testified against her, saying that Rebecca had asked, "Why do you bring her? She is one of us."

Fiske agreed to reconsider the matter, but when he returned to the jury room, none of the jurors could remember Rebecca's exact words. Fiske was given permission to question the prisoner, but when he asked her what she meant by her statement, the afflicted girls and the spectators were making so much noise that she did not hear his question. As she stared off into space, worn out from her ordeal, the embarrassed Fiske waited a little while, then returned to the jury room without the answer he had asked for. After polling the members once more, he reported to the Court that she was guilty as charged, and the Court sentenced her to be executed on July 19.

Her family petitioned Governor Phips, who had returned from Maine where he was directing the war against the Indians, to review her case, and he granted her a stay of execution until he could arrive at a decision. The members of the Court, several ministers, and the afflicted girls raised such an outcry when they learned of his interference, that Phips immediately rescinded the reprieve.

On July 3, at the morning service of the Salem church, the elders recommended that Rebecca Nurse be excommunicated, a recommendation that was approved by every member present. During the afternoon service, two constables escorted her, heavily manacled and bound with ropes, to the front of the church where she was forced to remain standing while the Reverend Mr. Nicholas Noyes read the words that made the deed official. After the lengthy ceremony was ended, she was returned to jail.

The following day, Thomas Fiske wrote an explanation of his actions for the record. "I, Thomas Fiske, the subscriber hereof, being one of them that were of the Jury last week at Salem-Court, upon the Tryal of Rebecca Nurse, etc., being desired by some of the Relations to give a reason why the Jury brought her in Guilty, after her verdict not Guilty; I do hereby give my reasons to be as follows, Viz:

"When the Verdict was not Guilty, the Honoured Court was pleased to object against it, saying to them, that they think they let slip the words, which the Prisoner at the Bar spake against herself, which were spoken in reply to Goodwife Hobbs and her daughter, who had been faulty in setting their hands to the Devil's Book, as they have confessed formerly; the words were, 'What, do these persons give in evidence against me now, they used to come among us.' After the honoured Court had manifested their dissatisfaction of the Verdict, several of the Jury declared themselves desirous to go out again, and thereupon the honoured Court gave leave; but when we came to consider of the Case, I could not tell how to take her words, as an Evidence against her, till she had a further opportunity to put her Sense upon them, if she would take it; and then going into Court, I mentioned the words aforesaid, which by one of the Court were affirmed to have been spoken by her, she being at the Bar, but made no reply, nor interpretation of them; whereupon these words were to me a principal Evidence against her.

Thomas Fiske."

Rebecca Nurse answered this in a Declaration to the Court. "These presents do humbly shew, to the honoured Court and Jury, that I being informed that the Jury had brought me in Guilty, upon my saying that Goodwife Hobbs and her Daughter were of our Company; but I intended no otherways than that they were Prisoners with us, and therefore did then and yet do judge them not legal Evidence against their fellow Prisoners. And I being somewhat hard of hearing and full of grief, none informing me how the Court took my words, and therefore had not the opportunity to declare what I intended, when I said they were of our Company.

Rebecca Nurse."

While she waited for the fateful day to arrive, Rebecca was visited by her family and several of her more courageous friends. They begged her to confess that she was a witch to save her life since confessed witches were not given the death penalty, but she refused to barter her soul for some extra time on earth.

On July 19, Rebecca Nurse and four other condemned witches were hanged on Gallows Hill in Salem. At sunset, their bodies were cut down, and buried on the rocky hill, since it was against the law to bury condemned witches in hallowed ground. Late that night, her sons disinterred her body, and brought it to the farm where they buried it in an unmarked grave. During the 19th century, a granite monument was erected to her memory on the approximate spot of her last resting place. On it are inscribed these words written by John Greenleaf Whittier:

"O Christian Martyr Who for Truth could die
When all about thee Owned the hideous lie!
The world, redeemed from superstition's sway,
Is breathing freer for thy sake to-day."

The Case of George Jacobs

The witchcraft persecutions affected few families as much as they did the Jacobs of Salem Village. Although George Jacobs, Sr. was the only one of the family to be executed, his son, daughter-in-law, and granddaughter were also accused of being witches. The last-named two were arrested and imprisoned, while George, Jr. fled from the jurisdiction of the court when he learned that the afflicted girls had named him as being one of their tormenters.

George, Sr. and his granddaughter Margaret were arrested on May 10, and Rebecca, Margaret's deranged mother, was arrested four days later. When George, Sr. was confronted by the afflicted girls during his examination at Corwin's house, he tended to treat the matter lightly during the first part of the questioning, laughing out loud at what he considered the absurdity of the questions. Asked why he was laughing, he answered that it was because he was amused by the humor of the false accusations. Hathorne, who was not in the least amused, turned to the girls to ask them if this was one of those who had tormented them. They answered that he was. Although Jacobs denied that he had hurt them, he was unable to tell the Magistrates who had done so. When another girl cried out that he had also tormented her, Jacobs realized how serious the situation actually was, and began to defend himself in earnest. He told the Magistrates that he was as innocent of the charges against him as a new-born baby, swearing that he had harmed no one during the 35 years he had lived in Salem Village.

His servant, Elizabeth Churchill, testified that he had appeared before her with a book which he asked her to sign, and Mary Walcott swore that he had threatened to harm her if she refused to sign the same book. Jacobs denied these allegations, again maintaining that he had lived a blameless life during his years in Salem Village. Hathorne's dispassionate voice cut his protestations short. "She accuses you to your face. She charges that you did hurt her twice. There are now three evidences against you." Jacobs at last lost his temper, and cried, "You tax me for a wizard, you may as well tax me for a buzzard. I have done no harm."

When Elizabeth Churchill advised her master to confess, Jacobs plaintively asked her if she had ever seen him perform any witchcraft. Pointing her finger at him, she said that he knew he was a wicked man, for he often refused to pray with his family. He admitted that this was true, but he did so only because he could neither read nor write. Elizabeth then told the court that during evening prayers Jacobs sometimes went out to the barn to work or sat on the back steps to smoke his pipe. The few times he did remain with his family, he was usually inattentive, and he sometimes even fell asleep.

Asked by Corwin to recite the Lord's Prayer, Jacobs became so agitated that he stumbled through his recitation, leaving out one whole sentence and garbling much of the rest of it. Seeing the looks of triumph on the faces of his accusers, he cried out in desperation, "Well burn me or hang me, I will stand in the truth of Christ."

The following day, Jacobs was again brought before his accusers to be examined, and the girls began to scream as soon as he entered the room. When one of the girls shouted that she felt as though she was being eviscerated, Jacobs was forced to touch each of the girls in turn so that the evil spirits would leave them and return to his body. Abigail Williams being asked if this man had ever hurt her, answered in the affirmative. Each of the other girls did the same when asked, and Jacobs was sent to jail to await trial.

Margaret was also sent to jail after a brief examination. During the weeks that elapsed before her grandfather's trial, Parris, the Magistrates, and some of the church elders were at her constantly to extract a confession from her. They explained in lurid detail the painful death that awaited her if she were found guilty in spite of her protestations of innocence, and the young girl's sleep was soon filled with nightmares. Under the cumulative effect of the overcrowded conditions of her jail cell, the importuning of her inquisitors, and the thought of facing the screaming girls in the courtroom, she at last broke down and confessed that she was indeed a witch, naming her grandfather, Constable John Willard, and the Reverend Mr. George Burroughs as fellow witches.

Her mother was already in jail, for she had been arrested late at night on May 14. She and her four remaining children were already asleep when a constable woke her and ordered her to follow him to Corwin's home for questioning. Although she protested that she was too tired to go anyplace, he assured her that she would be allowed to return home after the Magistrates were through with her. On the strength of this, she followed him to Corwin's house carrying her youngest child in her arms while the three older children trooped along behind, treating this serious matter as just another interesting disruption of their everyday lives.

When Rebecca entered Corwin's house, the afflicted girls at first failed to recognize her as one of their tormentors. This was to be expected, for she had had very little contact with her neighbors for several years. After some broad hints were dropped by the Magistrates, one girl at last cried out that this was "Jacobs, the old witch." The other girls immediately screamed that they were being tormented, and after a brief examination, the Magistrates sent her to jail to await her trial.

George Jacobs, Sr. was held in the Boston jail until August 5 when he was returned to Salem to be tried by the Court of Oyer and Terminer. Among those who testified against him were George Herrick, Mary Warren, Elizabeth Hubbard, Mary Walcott, Elizabeth Churchill, Sarah Bibber, John Doritch, Mercy Lewis, Joseph Flint, and his granddaughter Margaret.

Herrick testified that while the prisoner was in jail in Salem, he, the Jailer William Dounton, and Constable Joseph Neale, searched his body for any signs that might prove him to be a witch. He stated that "under the said Jacobs' right shoulder we found a pustule about a quarter inch long or better with a sharp point drooping downwards—I took a pin from said Dounton and ran it through the said pustule but there was neither water, blood, nor corruption nor any other matter and so we make return." Herrick added that Jacobs felt no pain when the pin was stuck through the eruption. In fact, he was not even aware of what had been done until the three men told him about it.

Depositions signed by the afflicted girls were entered as evidence against the old man, after which the obviously frightened Margaret testified against her grandfather. The jury finding Jacobs guilty as charged, the Court sentenced him to die on August 19. Five other persons were also condemned on this day: John and Elizabeth Proctor, John Willard, Martha Carrier, and George Burroughs. Since Elizabeth Proctor was pregnant, she was granted a stay of execution until after her child was born.

Because Margaret was now a confessed witch, she no longer shared a cell with those who were awaiting trial, but was held in another part of the jail with other confessors. Her living conditions were no better than they were before, but the daily examinations were ended, giving her ample time to reflect on what she had done. It was only now that she began to realize that her moral weakness was helping to send three innocent men to the gallows. After spending several sleepless nights in prayer and thought, she wrote to the Court of Oyer and Terminer retracting her testimoney and her confession. The Court would not grant the three men new trials on the basis of her retraction, but they ordered her placed with those awaiting trial, again. Now, she was again able to see her grandfather who was so pleased by her courageous action that he added a codicil to his will making Margaret one of his heirs. This was an empty gesture since the government seized the property of everyone convicted of witchcraft, and Jacobs would go to his death owning nothing but the clothing he wore, and even this could be stripped from him after he was dead. Jacobs advised Margaret to seek out Mr. Burroughs to ask his forgiveness. When she did, Burroughs not only forgave her, but knelt down and prayed for her.

On August 19, the five condemned prisoners, followed by a large crowd, were driven to Gallows Hill in an open cart. When Burroughs climbed the ladder, he preached a sermon for the benefit of those assembled to witness the executions, concluding it with a letter-perfect recitation of the Lord's Prayer. The people were so moved by the sermon and the prayer that a number of them pressed forward to demand that he be freed. Cotton Mather, sitting on a white horse, shouted to the crowd that Burroughs was not an ordained minister, and that the devil had aided him in his recital. Although it was commonly believed that neither the devil nor any of his followers could recite the Lord's Prayer without a mistake, his words calmed the crowd who allowed the hangman to complete his work. When the five were dead, they were buried in the rocky soil of the hill. The graves dug for them were so shallow that one had his chin and hand exposed, while another had his entire leg lying above the ground.

Margaret fainted when she received word that her grandfather was dead. The following day, after a sleepless night, the frightened and bewildered girl wrote to her father. The poignant letter reads:

From the Dungeon in Salem-Prison, August 20, 1692.

"Honoured Father,
    After my humble duty remembered to you, hoping in the Lord of your good health as blessed be God I enjoy, tho in abundance of affliction, being close confined here in a loathsome dungeon; the Lord look down in mercy upon me, not knowing how soon I shall be put to death, by means of the afflicted persons, my grandfather having suffered already, and all his estate seized for the king. The reason of my confinement is this: I having through the magistrates' threatenings, and my own vile and wretched heart, confessed several things contrary to my conscience and knowledge, though to the wounding of my soul, (the Lord pardon me for it!) but oh, the terrors of a wounded conscience who can bear? But blessed be the Lord, he would not let me go on in my sins, but in mercy, I hope, to my soul, would not suffer me to keep it any longer; but I was forced to confess the truth of all before the magistrates, who would not believe me, but it is their pleasure to put me in here, and God knows how soon I shall be put to death. Dear Father, let me beg your prayers to the Lord on my behalf, and send us a joyful and happy

meeting in heaven. My mother, poor woman, is very crazy, and remembers her kind love to you and to uncle viz: D. A. So leaving you to the protection of the Lord, I rest your dutiful daughter.

Margaret Jacobs"

Margaret was scheduled to be tried in September, but she was so ill on the scheduled date that the authorities postponed her trial, and before a new date could be set, the Governor ordered all those prisoners who could pay their board bills and their court costs to be freed. Since the colony had seized her grantfather's and her father's properties, she was unable to raise any money, and she remained in jail until a stranger, learning of her plight, loaned her the necessary money, a loan she later repaid in full.

The Ordeal of Philip English

The wealthiest merchant in Salem during the witchcraft hysteria was Philip English, a native of Jersey, one of the British-owned Channel Islands that lie just off the coast of France. He emigrated to Salem just prior to 1670 where he became the friend and protege of William Hollingsworth, one of the most influential merchants of the town, and five years later he married Mary, his benefactor's only child.

By 1686, English owned a fleet of 21 ships, had shares in many more, owned his own wharf and a huge warehouse, owned fourteen buildings throughout the town, and had just built a beautiful mansion on Essex Street where he lived with his young family. Neither Philip nor Mary had any desire to become embroiled in the witchcraft persecutions. They were content to devote their complete attention to their business and personal affairs.

Mary was well aware that the fact that she and Philip were Episcopalians might draw an unwelcome attention to them, so she applied for permission to join the First Church of Salem. She had already made her Covenant and been baptized with her children, and she expected to be received as a member at the Communion on Sunday, April 19, 1692.

At 11:00 P.M. on Saturday, April 18, Sheriff George Corwin and several of his deputies came to the English house with a warrant for Mary's arrest. Going to her bedchamber, he opened the curtains around her bed, and ordered her to accompany him. Mary refused to do so, telling him that he could return in the morning to arrest her. Cowed by her imperious tone, Corwin agreed to this, but he ordered his men to surround the house so that she could not escape during the night. Early the following morning he returned to advise her that it was time to leave, but she told him that it was much too early, and that she would arise at her regular hour.

When she did get up, she first joined her family at breakfast, made her farewells to the twenty servants she employed, then instructed her husband how she wished the children to be educated. When she had attended to all these duties, she called Corwin into the house and told him that she was now ready to die.

Instead of taking her to jail as he would a person of lesser importance, Corwin brought her to the Cat and Wheel, a tavern near the meeting house, where he kept her locked in a second-floor room. This was directly above the room in which a number of examinations were held, and the fact that only a single layer of boards separated the two floors made it possible for her to hear almost every word spoken during the examinations of other suspects.

Philip, who visited her three times a day, was becoming increasingly outspoken in his criticism and condemnation of the afflicted persons (a number of men and boys were now included in the group), and as had happened so many times before in similar cases, a warrant was issued for his arrest on April 30. Mary had overheard enough to know that this was going to happen, and she convinced him to flee from the jurisdiction of the Court before it was served so the children would have at least one parent to raise them.

Unwilling to completely abandon Mary and the children, Philip at first hid in a secret room in his house, then went to Boston where he tried to use his influence to have Mary freed. When he was unable to do so, he began to worry that his continued absence would affect Mary's case adversely, so he surrendered to the Salem authorities. He was examined at Salem Village on May 31, and the Magistrates were so convinced of his guilt that they ordered him taken to jail to await his trial. Through the intercession of friends, they were sent to the jail in Boston where the jailer, probably under orders from the Governor, allowed the couple to travel freely about the town during the day, although they slept at the prison each night.

On the day before they were to be returned to Salem to be tried, the young couple attended a public worship at the First Church of Boston conducted by the Reverend Mr. Joshua Moody and the Reverend Mr. Samuel Willard. Moody had chosen Mathew 10:23 as his text: "When they persecute you in one town, flee to another," and after the services were ended, both ministers visited the Englishes at the jail. Asking if they had paid attention to the sermon, the ministers warned them that they would lose their lives if they allowed themselves to be tried, urging them to go to New York until the madness in Salem was ended. They explained that there was a precedent in Scriptures for this, since this was the advice Jesus had given his disciples when he sent them out to gather together the lost sheep of Israel.

English did not want to leave, claiming that God would not allow anything to happen to them because they were innocent. Mary, more realistic than her husband, asked if he did not think that the other prisoners were innocent. When he answered in the affirmative, she asked, "Why may we not suffer, also?" English was at last convinced that he and Mary would be safe only if they left Massachusetts.

Late that night, Philip and Mary English began the long overland journey to New York in a carriage donated by one of their friends. They brought their two oldest children with them as well as letters of introduction from Governor Phips to Governor Fletcher of New York. They remained as his guests for one year before they returned to Salem. During their stay they learned of the suffering of the poor in Salem—there was a scarcity of food caused by a protracted drought and the fact that so many people neglected their farms to attend the examinations and trials, afraid that their absence might focus attention on them. To help these people, English sent a shipload of corn to Salem, enough to give a bushel to every needy person in the town.

In 1693, when the hysteria was over, English returned to Salem over the protests of Governor Fletcher and other friends they had made in New York. A day of thanksgiving was proclaimed by the Salem church when they returned, the Reverend Mr. Nicholas Noyes being one of those who entertained them to celebrate their repatriation. Once the celebrations were over, Philip and Mary learned that Sheriff George Corwin, acting under orders from Deputy Governor Stoughton, had confiscated much of their personal property, estimated to be worth between 1100 and 1500 pounds sterling. Corwin was so thorough that the only furniture they found in their beautiful new home was a cot in the servants' quarters.

Mary's health was severely damaged by her ordeal and by the work needed to reorganize their affairs, and she died shortly after she gave birth to a son in 1694. Philip returned to his shipping, continuing in this business until his death in 1736. He appealed to the Superior Court for redress in 1694, claiming that his property had been seized illegally and naming George Corwin as the person responsible for his losses. Most of the costs of prosecuting and caring for those accused of witchcraft during the hysteria had been borne by the money raised from selling the properties of English and those of other suspects that were also seized. Since the province's treasury was at this time unable to raise the money to repay him, the plea was denied.

In spite of this, English continued to petition for redress, and in 1711 the General Court set aside a small sum to reimburse a growing number of claimants. The entire sum was about 532 pounds sterling, less than half of what was owed English. Because of the frequent outbursts of temper he directed toward those committee members who were appointed by the General Court to disburse the money, he did not receive any of it. After his death, the General Court granted his heirs damages of 200 pounds sterling in full settlement of the losses he sustained in 1692.

A number of stories were circulated in the 18th and 19th centuries about English, one of them about how he finally managed a revenge of sorts against Sheriff George Corwin. This one stated that when Corwin died in 1696 at the age of thirty, English seized his body and would not release it until his family ransomed it for approximately 60 pounds. There is no truth to this story, but there is for another which is even more dramatic. Since Corwin was the official hangman and the most visible member of the law-enforcement team in power during the hysteria, it is only natural that the relatives and friends of those who were persecuted during that period would direct most of their venom at him, many of them charging that he enjoyed carrying out what to a more normal person would have been distasteful duties. Resentment against him was still so high when he died that his family buried him in the cellar of his own home to prevent the almost-certain desecration of his remains if he were buried in the cemetery. This was hardly a fitting end for a dedicated public servant who was also the great grandson of Governor John Winthrop.

Although English eventually rebuilt his financial empire, the ordeal of 1692/1693 and the loss of his beloved Mary colored his actions for the remainder of his life. He made no secret of the fact that he despised the people who had caused his family so much suffering, particularly George Corwin and Magistrate John Hathorne. He refused to forgive Hathorne until just before he died, doing so then only because he felt obliged to do so as a Christian. An interesting sidelight is the fact that the two families were finally brought together by the marriage of a Hathorne to an English. This union produced a line of men whose most famous member was Nathaniel Hawthorne, the literary great who was born on July 4, 1804. Shortly after he was graduated from college, his older sister convinced him that their side of the family should alter their name to separate them from the others, and it was he who added the "w" that changed it to "Hawthorne."

Giles and Martha Cory

THE MAN OF IRON

Giles Cory was a wizard strong, a stubborn wretch was he;
And fit was he to hang on high upon the locust tree.

So, when before the Magistrates for trial he did come,
He would no true confession make, but was completely dumb.

"Giles Cory," said the Magistrate, "What hast thou here to plead
To those who now accuse thy soul of crime and horrid deed?"

Giles Cory he said not a word, no single word spoke he.
"Giles Cory," said the Magistrate, "We'll press it out of thee."

They got them then a heavy beam, then laid it on his breast;
They loaded it with heavy stones, and hard upon him prest.

"More weight!" now said this wretched man, "More weight!" again he cried;
And he did no confession make, but wickedly he died.

The above poem, written sometime in the early years of the 18th century by an unknown author, is a tribute to Giles Cory, a simple, uneducated, 80-year-old farmer who has the distinction of being the only man in our history who was ever legally pressed to death.

Giles and his wife Martha, members of the Salem Church, were among those who attended the examinations of the first suspects. While he believed in witches and evil spirits and was eager to listen to every bit of testimony presented at the examinations, Martha, like Rebecca Nurse, was sceptical about the sincerity of the accusations of the afflicted girls, and made the mistake of airing her doubts in public. Once the girls learned of her attacks against them, they accused her of afflicting them. Ann Putnam, Jr. claimed that she had seen Martha with other witches, and that Martha had tormented her on a number of occasions.

Because of Martha's unimpeachable reputation for piety, the authorities did not want to arrest her unless the evidence was overwhelmingly against her, so Edward Putnam and Ezekiel Cheevers were sent out to the Cory farm to question her. Because Ann Putnam, Jr. had claimed to see Martha's spectre on several different occasions, the men asked her a number of questions before they went to interview Martha, one of them concerning the clothing that Martha was then wearing. The child was too clever to be caught in a trap, and she told the men that she could not answer this question since the witches had temporarily taken away her spectral vision.

When the two men arrived at the Cory farm, Martha greeted them cordially. She told them that she knew why they were there, and when she told them that she knew that they had asked Ann to describe the clothes she was wearing, the two were convinced that she was indeed a witch. Her statement that no witches were operating against the church, and that that the devil had sent the girls to harm the community only served to strengthen their belief that she was guilty as charged. On their recommendation, a warrant for her arrest was issued on Saturday, March 19, although it was not served until the following Monday when she was brought to the meeting house where her examination was preceded by a long prayer by Nicholas Noyes. When she asked permission to follow this with a prayer of her own, she was told that the Magistrates were there to question her, not to hear her pray.

Hathorne began the questioning by asking her why she afflicted the girls, pointing to those who had accused her (Ann Putnam, Sr., Ann Putnam, Jr., Mercy Lewis, Abigail Williams, and Elizabeth Hubbard), to which she replied that she did not torment them in any way. When he asked her who did hurt them, she told him she did not know who it might be. The girls now started to scream, saying that she was biting, scratching, and strangling them. They claimed that her apparition was holding out a book for them to sign, but Martha said this was not so for she had never seen a book such as they described.

One girl shouted that Martha had a yellow bird suckling between her fingers, and when Hathorne told Martha to explain this, she said she knew nothing about a yellow bird. She insisted that she was a Gospel woman, but the girls shouted that she was a Gospel Witch.

Ann Putnam, Jr. testified that on one occasion when Lieutenant Fuller was at her house to take part in evening prayers with her family, she looked out the window and saw Goodwives Cory and Nurse praying to the devil. Martha now became angry, and told Hathorne that no attention should be paid to any of these girls as it was plain that they were distracted. Reverend Noyes curtly informed her that she was the only person who thought they were distracted, for everyone else was convinced that they were bewitched.

The afflicted girls frequently interrupted the proceedings by their agonized screams. When Martha bit her lip to help her concentrate on a particularly difficult question, one of the girls ran to the Magistrates to show them the blood streaming from her own lips, swearing that Martha had bitten her. If Martha clasped her hands together, the girls shouted that she was pinching them, and if she moved her feet, they began stamping their own feet as if to drive the pain away. Gertrude Pope seemed to suffer more than the rest, for she claimed that she felt as though her bowels were being torn out. When the pain was at its worst, she threw her muff at Martha, and when it missed its mark, she took off a shoe and struck the old woman on the side of the head with it.

One of the girls asked Martha why she did not join the rest of the witches who were then assembling across the street beside Ingersoll's Tavern. Another told the magistrates that the Black Man had remained at Martha's side throughout most of the examination, whispering advice to her when the Magistrates questioned her, while one girl testified that Martha had signed a ten-year pact with the devil that had four more years to go before it was over.

Hathorne asked Martha several questions from the Catechism, all of which she answered correctly. In spite of this, he and Corwin ordered her taken to jail in Salem in await trial, and when the Salem jail later became too crowded to hold all those suspected of witchcraft, she was one of those transferred to the one in Boston.

Giles had been called to the witness stand at her examination, at which time he mentioned several uncommon accidents that had occurred in his home since he married her (she was his second wife). It was not until he returned home that he realized that the Magistrates might have attributed these accidents to Martha's malevolence. Since he was certain that she was as innocent as he, he began to speak out against the girls as strongly as she had. As he probably suspected would happen, some of the girls cried out against him, and a warrant was issued for his arrest on April 19. Mary Warren, Bridget Bishop, and Abigail Hobbs were also arrested on this date, while several more suspects, among them William and Deliverance Hobbs, Abigail's parents, were arrested on April 21.

When Abigail was examined, she readily confessed that she was a witch, and accused Giles Cory, among others, of being part of a coven that was planning to destroy the Salem Church. Her mother also confessed that she was a witch, naming a large number of fellow-conspirators who planned to destroy both the First Church of Salem and the parish church at Salem Village, one of whom was Giles Cory. The Magistrates, convinced of Cory's guilt, ordered him taken to jail to await his trial.

Several depositions were introduced as evidence against him at his trial on September 19, most of them being similar in content. Ann Putnam, Jr. deposed that on April 13 his apparition appeared before her with a large book which he ordered her to sign. He beat her when she refused to do so, reappearing with the book periodically after this until April 19. His spectre continued to torment her even after he was in jail, and it once choked her until she thought he would succeed in killing her.

Mercy Lewis stated that Cory beat her so often and so vigorously because she refused to sign the book that she was certain he had damaged her back. Sarah Bibber claimed she saw him torment several of the younger girls, and that he also whipped her on a number of occasions. Mary Warren swore that he whipped her several times, while Elizabeth Woodwell and Mary Walcott claimed that they saw Giles at church services the Sunday before Bridget Bishop was hanged, saying that he remained seated throughout the services, then walked outside with the other men without any of them suspecting that he was there.

Benjamin Gould attested that Giles and Martha Cory visited his bedside on April 6, stared at him for some time without speaking, and then left. He later found two bruises on his side that had not been there before. Another time he met Giles and John Proctor while both were in jail, and they caused his left foot to pain so much that he was unable to wear a boot on that foot for three days.

Susannah Sheldon accused Giles of having murdered his first wife, stating that he would also have murdered Martha except for the fact that she too was a witch. A 16-year-old boy testified that Giles borrowed some platters from him on August 20 that were to be used at a witches' feast. He brought them back 30 minutes later, then left without uttering a word. Elizabeth Booth swore that Giles was one of a gathering of 50 witches at Salem Village who were taking part in a Black Sabbat. When Cory saw her, he brought her some bread and wine so she could share in the devil's sacrament then beat her with a stick when she refused to take any.

After these depositions were read, Cory was brought to the stand and asked how he pleaded. He remained mute, knowing that under English Common Law he could not be tried for any crime except for high treason until he entered a plea. Chief Justice Stoughton ordered Sherrif Corwin to take the old man to the field next to the court house, stake him to the ground on his back, then place weights on him until he agreed to enter a plea. This was the "peine forte et dure" of England applied to those who refused to enter a plea at their own trials. These prisoners were taken to a cell, placed on their backs, and had more and heavier weights placed on them until they either agreed to be placed under the protection of the common law or were crushed to death.

Corwin and his deputies brought him out to the field, staked him to the ground, placed a heavy beam on his body, then piled several large rocks on the beam. When Cory stubbornly refused to speak, Corwin ordered his men to gather more rocks. These were also added to the others, but Cory courageously refused to utter a word until he felt the bones of his ribs cracking. He then pleaded with the sheriff to add more weight on him so he could die more quickly. The deputies added so much more that Cory's tongue was forced out of his mouth as the life left his body. Corwin callously pushed it back with the end of his cane, then ordered his men to bury him in an unmarked grave on Gallows Hill.

Eleven convicted witches were executed between the day Cory was arrested and the day he was tried. Knowing that the Court of Oyer and Terminer had found everyone brought before it guilty, and that the Crown had confiscated the properties of each of these, Cory decided to remain mute at his trial. He made out a will leaving his entire property to his sons-in-law, and although the government later contested his will, the courts were forced to find in favor of his heirs since he had not been found guilty of the charges against him.

On September 22, Martha Cory, Mary Eastey, Alice Parker, Mary Parker, Ann Pudeator, Margaret Scott, Wilmot Redd, and Samuel Wardwell were taken from their cells in the Salem jail and placed in a cart that was to take them to Gallows Hill to be hanged. As the horses were pulling the cart up the hill, the wheels froze so that the horses were unable to pull it any farther for some time. The afflicted girls shouted that the devil was trying to hinder the execution of his people, but several men pushed against the cart until it started up again, thereby thwarting the devil's scheme.

Samuel Wardwell began to pray before he was hanged, but he was forced to stop when smoke from the hangman's pipe blew into his face and choked him. Martha Cory also prayed before she was hanged, but she allowed nothing to interrupt her. When the eight were all dead, and before they were cut down and burried somewhere on the hill, Nicholas Noyes pointed to them and remarked that it was a sad thing to see "eight firebrands of hell hanging there." These were the last of those convicted of witchcraft who were hanged during the hysteria.

The Case of John Alden of Boston

John Alden of Boston, the 70-year-old son of Priscilla (Mullins) and John Alden of Plymouth who were immortalized by Longfellow in the "Courtship of Myles Standish," had fought against the Indians in his younger years and had amassed a fortune as a fur trader and the owner of several merchant ships that made him one of the wealthiest men in Massachusetts. In spite of his wealth and renown, or maybe because of it, the afflicted girls at Salem Village cried out against him sometime in May, accusing him of being the leader of the Boston witches.

Alden received word on May 28 through Deputy Governor William Stoughton that he was to appear at Salem Village on the morning of May 31 to answer to the charges against him. Alden arrived there late in the morning of the appointed day. As soon as he arrived, he went directly to the meeting house where Hathorne, Corwin, and Bartholomew Gedney, the three Salem Magistrates, had just completed the examination of another suspect.

When he entered the courtroom, the afflicted girls were screaming that they were being tortured by witches, some of them rolling about the floor in their agony while others were twisting their bodies into strange, unnatural positions. Hathorne asked them to name those who were afflicting them, but none of them was able to answer him, the witches having temporarily taken away their powers of speech.

Although the afflicted girls knew that Alden was scheduled to appear for questioning that day, none of them had ever seen him, and when they were pressed by Hathorne to identify the person who was tormenting them, Abigail Williams pointed wordlessly to a man dressed in the same kind of seaman's clothing worn by Alden. Since this was obviously the wrong person, a man standing behind her—although he was not identified, it is certain that he was either Nicholas Noyes or Samuel Parris—bent down to whisper in her ear, after which she cried out that it was Alden who was tormenting her. When Hathorne asked her to point him out, she admitted that she was unable to do so since she had never seen him. Asked how she knew it was Alden who was hurting her, she answered that the "man" had told her.

In order to get a positive identification, the Magistrates ordered everyone outside to the front of the meeting house where a circle was formed around the suspect. Abigail now cried out, "There stands Alden, a bold fellow with his hat on before the Judges. He sells powder and shot to the French and the Indians, lies with the Indian squaws, and has Indian papooses." Since he had been identified, he was turned over to the Marshall who immediately confiscated his sword, the girls having complained that he was cutting and pinching them with it. Several hours later, he was again brought to the meeting house where he was ordered to stand on a chair before the Magistrates. Because the girls complained that he could hurt them by clenching his fists, the Marshall and a constable remained at his side throughout the entire examination to make certain that he kept his hands open.

Alden was pleased to see that Bartholomew Gedney, a close personal friend of many years, was present, feeling that Gedney would vouch for him and convince his colleagues to drop the ridiculous charges against him. After Hathorne asked him why he had hurt the girls in the past and continued to hurt them, Alden asked Gedney if he and the other Magistrates believed he had nothing better to do than to come to a small, little-known village to torture children he had never seen before. Instead of answering him directly, Gedney advised him to confess his guilt and glorify God. Alden, who was a deeply religious person, replied that he would always glorify God, although he would not do so merely to gratify the devil. Turning to the spectators, he begged those who knew him to step forward and testify to the fact that he had always been a sincere, upright Christian, challenging any person present to present proof that he had ever indulged in any form of wizardry. None of the spectators came to his defense, but Gedney spoke up saying that he had known Alden for many years, had even served aboard ship with him, and although he had always considered Alden to be an honest, God-fearing man, he now saw reason to change his opinion.

After Gedney had finished speaking, Hathorne ordered Alden to look at the girls. When he did so, each of them again fell to the floor, screaming that Alden was hurting them. Gedney triumphantly pointed to this as proof of Alden's guilt.

When he could be heard above the noise, Alden asked Gedney why it was that only those few girls were affected by his look, maintaining that if he were truly in the devil's service every person he looked at, including the three Magistrates, would be equally affected. Instead of answering, Gedney ordered Alden to touch each of the girls to relieve them of their pains.

This struck Alden as such an absurdity that he angrily shouted that God's providence was being abused by allowing these wicked children to accuse innocent persons of such a serious crime. Nicholas Noyes interrupted him to say that he had no right to question God's providence, asserting that through His providence God governed and kept peace in the entire world. He went on in this same vein for some time, the Magistrates allowing him to continue until he finished what he wanted to say.

When it became obvious to Alden that his guilt had been established long before he arrived at the meeting house, he told the Magistrates that the girls were either liars or were under the influence of a lying spirit, for there was no truth to any of the charges against him. His impassioned outburst had no effect on the verdict, however, for the Magistrates ordered the Marshall to take him to jail in Boston where he was to be held until his trial. The order read:

"To Mr. John Arnold, Keeper of the Prison in Boston, in the County of Suffolk:

"Wheras Captain John Alden of Boston, Mariner, and Sarah Rice, wife of NIcholas Rice of Reading, husbandman, have been this day brought before us, John Hathorne and Jonathan Corwin, Esquires; being accused and suspected of perpetrating divers acts of Witchcraft, contrary to the form of the Statute, in that case made and provided: These are therefore in Their Majesties, King William and Queen Mary's Names, to Will and require you to take into your Custody, the bodies of the said John Alden and Sarah Rice, and them safely keep, until they shall thence be delivered by due course of Law; as you will answer the contrary at your peril; and this shall be your sufficient Warrant, Given under our hands at Salem Village the 31st of May, in the Fourth Year of the Reign of our Sovereign Lord and Lady, William and Mary, now King and Queen over England, etc., Anno Dom. 1692.

John Hathorne
Jonathan Corwin, Assistants."

A number of his friends, among them three ministers—Cotton Mather, James Allen, and Samuel Willard—two sea captains, and Samuel Sewall, one of the justices on the special Court of Oyer and Terminer, held a solemn day of fasting and prayer at his house on July 20. Some of these same people visited him at the jail shortly afterward to argue that he could only be safe if he fled out of the jurisdiction of the Court. He stubbornly refused to leave at first, but after spending 15 weeks chained in his cell, he was convinced, and allowed his friends to bribe the jailers and provide a carriage to take him to New York.

He remained in New York until the following April, returning to Boston almost a month before Governor Phips issued his proclamation. He was tried at the April 25 sitting of the Superior Court, and when no witnesses appeared against him, he was set free.

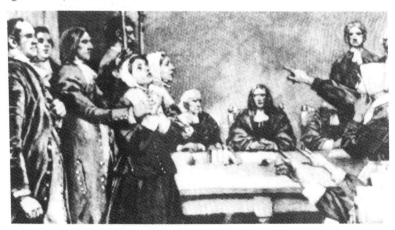

Epilogue

Once Salem and Salem Village had rid themselves of most of their witches, the people of several towns asked to borrow the afflicted girls to help ferret out those living in their own communities. Within a short time, the girls had uncovered a large number of suspects. In Andover alone more than 50 were arrested with their help. As their fame grew, however, the girls became more daring, crying out against several highly-placed people, among them the Reverend Mr. John Hale's wife, Judge Corwin's mother-in-law, and Governor Phips's wife. When Phips returned from Maine, he was told of these accusations. Although he had not wanted to become involved in the proceedings, he studied the cases of those already executed, finding out when he did so that everyone of them had been convicted on the basis of spectral evidence, contrary to the recommendations of the committee of twelve ministers. Because of this, he disbanded the Court of Oyer and Terminer.

The General Court created the Superior Court the following month, and with Lt. Governor Stoughton still acting as Chief Justice, it sat at Salem on January 3, 1692/93. Since by Executive order the Court could no longer accept spectral evidence against any of the defendants, of the 52 persons tried at this sitting, 49 were cleared when it was found that the cases against them were predicated on this inadmissable evidence. The angry Stoughton, hoping to execute the three who were found guilty before there was any further interference from the Governor, signed their death warrants as well as those of five others who had previously been found guilty by the Court of Oyer and Terminer but who had been granted reprieves for one reason or another.

When the Governor learned of this, he immediately signed a stay of execution for the eight. Stoughton was so angered by this that he refused to sit with the Court when it moved to Charlestown. He exclaimed, "We were in a way to have cleared the land of these creatures. Who it is that obstructs the course of justice I know not; the Lord be merciful to the country."

One of the cases heard by the Superior Court at Charlestown was that of Sarah Daston whose neighbors had suspected her of being a witch for almost 30 years. Her trial drew huge crowds from Boston and the other nearby towns, most of whom hoped that the jury would eliminate this threat to their well-being by condemning her. In spite of her unpopularity, she was found not guilty, as were her daughter and grand-daughter who were also tried at this time. Although she was technically free to resume her life, she had to remain in prison until her jail and court costs were paid, but she died before her family could raise the necessary funds.

When the Superior Court moved to Boston to clear the back log of cases in that town, Deputy Governor Stoughton presided at the session which began on April 25. At this sitting, Mary Watkins, a servant girl, was to be tried. She had once stated that her mistress was a witch, but when the woman threatened to punish her if she persisted in talking in this fashion, she retracted her statement. Mary, who had been ill for some time prior to her accusation, suffered a relapse after this that left her so despondent that she tried to strangle herself. While she was recovering from this misadventure, she confessed that she was a witch, and she was sent to jail to await her trial. The evidence against her was so flimsy that the jury quickly returned a finding of not guilty. Stoughton asked the foreman to reconsider this verdict just as he had in the case of Rebecca Nurse, but the jury, refusing to be browbeaten into a wrong decision, again returned with a finding of not guilty. Unable to pay her jail and court costs, she remained in jail until a Virginia planter bought her by paying the money she owed.

Governor Phips had written to England for advice when he returned from Maine in October, and in May the long-awaited reply arrived, a reply that convinced him that there was no further need to continue the witch trials. He immediately issued a proclamation pardoning everyone who was in jail and granting amnesty to those who had fled from the jurisdiction of the Court to escape prosecution, thereby officially ending the witchcraft hysteria of 1692.

*   *   *

Governor Phips was ordered back to England in 1694 to answer to charges that he had misappropriated government funds. He died in 1695, several weeks after he arrived in London. William Stoughton served as acting Governor from the time of Phips's departure until 1698 when the new Governor arrived. Seeing that many of the Massachusetts colonists suffered from pangs of conscience, he issued a Proclamation on December 17, 1696 which stated, "Wherefore, it is commanded and appointed, that Thursday, the 14th of January next be observed as a Day of Prayer with Fasting throughout the Province, strictly forbidding all servile labor thereon; that so all God's people may offer up fervent supplications . . . that all iniquity may be put away which hath stirred God's Holy jealously against this land; That he would . . . help us wherein we have done amiss to do so no more; and especially that whatever mistakes on either hand have been fallen into . . . referring to the late tragedy, raised among us by Satan and his instruments, through the awful judgment of God, he would humble us therefor and pardon all the errors of his servants and people that desire to love his name and be attuned to this land; that he would remove the rod of the wicked from off the lot of the righteous; that he would bring the American heathen, and cause them to hear and obey his voice."

On that January 14, Judge Samuel Sewall attended services at the South Church. He handed Mr. Willard a paper to read to the congregation, and remained standing until the minister was finished. It read, "Samuel Sewall, sensible of the reiterated strokes of God upon himself and his family, and being sensible that as to the guilt contracted upon the opening of the late Commission of Oyer and Terminer at Salem . . . he is, upon many accounts, more concerned than any that he knows of, desires to take the blame and shame of it, asking pardon of men, and especially desiring prayers that God . . . would pardon that sin and all other his sins . . . (and) not visit the sin of him, or of any other, upon himself or any of his, nor upon the land: But that he would powerfully defend him against any temptations to sin for the future; and vouchsafe him the efficacious saving conduct of his word and Spirit." He observed a day of humiliation and prayer each year on this date for the rest of his life.

The Salem jurors also circulated a paper that year in which they admitted that "they were not capable to understand nor to withstand the mysterious delusion of the powers of darkness", and they humbly begged the forgiveness of everyone who had been harmed by their actions.

That same year, John Hale wrote a thorough report of his personal experiences during the hysteria. In it he mentioned some of his former doubts concerning the guilt of several suspected witches, and marvelled at the manner in which the list of afflicted persons grew so rapidly. His was more an admission of an error in judgment than the "mea culpas" of Seward and the jurors.

As the hysteria abated, Rebecca Nurse's children led a revolt against Samuel Parris's leadership, openly demanding that he resign. When Parris refused to do so, many of the insurgents stopped attending services and refused to pay their tithes. Most of the Farmers could ill aford to do so, anyway. Not only had the area suffered one of its worst droughts in memory in 1692, but many of the people had neglected their farms in order to attend the various examinations and trials.

Citing these and other reasons, members of the Salem Village church petitioned the General Court for permission to stop paying Parris's salary, but although the Court refused to honor their request, Parris was unable to collect his entire salary for the remainder of his stay in Salem Village. In 1694, realizing that he would have to take heroic measures to heal the rift in the membership, he publicly apologized for his actions during the hysteria, but when this did not have the desired effect, he pleaded for help from Increase and Cotton Mather and the leading ministers of the North Shore. At a meeting held in Salem, the Mathers convinced the other ministers to recommend that the parishioners completely forget the past, and unite behind Parris in true Christian fellowship.

Ignoring the recommendations, the parishioners continued to press for his resignation. Parris's wife, who had recently given birth to ther second child, a boy named Noyes after the Associate Minister of the Salem Church, died in 1696, and Parris resigned his post the year after she died. He and his two children first went to Boston where he entered the field of trade for a short time, after which he again returned to the pulpit, his last ministry being at Sudbury where he died in 1720.

The Reverend Mr. Joseph Greene, his successor at Salem Village, was an earnest young man who was able to restore the principles of Christian charity in the members of his church. He was so successful that they were able to forgive Ann Putnam, Jr. when she humbled herself at church services shortly after he assumed his duties.

The General Court in 1711 divided the sum of 532 pounds sterling among those who had suffered during the hysteria, and the following year the Salem Church set aside the excommunications of Rebecca Nurse and Giles Cory, the last meaningful acts bearing on the witchcraft hysteria of 1692.

Pre-trial examinations were held in a number of places. Some were held at Jonathan Corwin's home in Salem, several at Thomas Beadle's tavern in Salem, a much larger number at Ingersoll's tavern in Salem Village, and the great majority were held at the meeting house in Salem Village. When the examinations were held at the meeting house, a table and bench were placed up front close to the wall. This is where the Magistrates sat as they presided over the proceedings. The afflicted girls and others who served as witnesses for the Crown sat in the first two pews in the right-hand section of the building, while the prisoners, always accompanied by one or more constables, stood in front of the witnesses and the Magistrates. In some cases there was no actual prisoner's bar, although the minister's high-backed chair, turned around, was usually pressed into service as a bar.

WITCHCRAFT NOTES

Victims of the Hysteria

June 10
Bridget Bishop of Salem

July 19
Sarah Good, Salem Village
Rebecca Nurse, Salem Village
Susannah Martin, Amesbury
Elizabeth How, Ipswich
Sarah Wildes, Topsfield

August 19
George Burroughs, Wells, Maine
John Proctor, Salem Village
John Willard, Salem Village
George Jacobs, Salem
Martha Carrier, Andover

September 19
Giles Cory, Salem Farms, pressed to death

September 22
Martha Cory, Salem Farms
Mary Eastey, Topsfield
Alice Parker, Salem
Ann Pudeater, Salem
Margaret Scott, Rowley
Wilmet Redd, Marblehead
Samuel Wardwell, Andover
Mary Parker, Andover

COURT OF OYER AND TERMINER

Deputy Governor William Stoughton, Chief Justice
Associate Justices
Captain Samuel Sewall
William Sergeant, Boston
Wait Winthrop, Boston
Bartolomew Gedney, Salem
John Richards, Boston
Major Nathaniel Saltonstall, Haverhill
*Jonathan Corwin

*Corwin replaced Saltonstall when the latter resigned his post in June, 1692.

THE JURY SITTING AT SALEM

Thomas Fisk, Foreman
William Fisk
John Bacheler
Thomas Fisk, Jr.
John Dane
Joseph Evelith
Thomas Perly, Sr.
John Pebody
Thomas Perkins
Samuel Sayer
Andrew Elliot
Henry Herrick, Sr.

Clerk of Court, Stephen Sewall

King's Attorney, Thomas Newton

Magistrates

Jonathan Corwin
John Hathorne

High Sheriff

George Corwin

THE AFFLICTED GIRLS

Elizabeth Parris 9, daughter of Samuel Parris

Abigail Williams 11, neice of Samuel Parris

Ann Putnam, Jr. 12, daughter of Thomas and Ann Putnam

Ann Putnam, Sr.

Elizabeth Hubbard 18, niece and servant of Dr. Griggs

Mary Warren 17, servant of John Proctor

Mercy Lewis 19, servant of Thomas Putnam

Mary Walcott 16, daughter of Captain Jonathan Walcott

Sarah Bibber 36

Elizabeth Booth 16

Mrs. Gertrude Pope, a wealthy middle-aged matron

Elizabeth Churchill 20, servant of George Jacobs, Sr., and
Susannah Sheldon 18.

Procedure Used in the Witchcraft Cases

1. The afflicted person complained to the Magistrates about a suspect, sometimes doing so through another person.

2. A warrant was issued for the arrest of the accused.

3. The accused was examined by two or more Magistrates. If the Magistrates were convinced that the accused was guilty, he was sent to jail where he was usually reexamined.

4. The case of the accused was presented to the Grand Jury at which time depositions were introduced as evidence by the accusers.

5. If the accused was indicted by the Grand Jury, he was tried before a jury sitting with the Court of Oyer and Terminer.

6. If the jury found the defendant guilty, the Court passed sentence, in each case the defendant was sentenced to die by hanging at a specified date.

7. The Sheriff and his deputies carried out the sentence on the day appointed by the Court.

* * *

During the first few weeks of the hysteria, the afflicted girls constantly complained that they were still being tormented by the spectres of the accused witches who were in jail, inferring that this was because these prisoners were allowed complete freedom of movement. When Sir William Phips arrived in Boston on May 14 to assume his duties as Royal Governor of Massachusetts, one of his first official acts was to order the prisoners shackled. The girls stopped complaining after this, unaware that several of the more humane jailers kept most of their prisoners in irons only when they feared a visit from the ministers or one of the higher-ranking authorities, allowing them the same freedom they had enjoyed before Phips's edict.

* * *

There were a number of reasons why people "cried out" against the accused witches. Some did it to direct suspicion away from themselves, others enjoyed the feeling of importance this part in the tragedy gave them, while still others did it for revenge for real or imagined wrongs done to them or their families in the past.

* * *

Lt. Governor William Stoughton was educated for the ministry at Harvard from where he was graduated with the class of 1650. He then accepted a call from a small church in England while he studied for and received his Master's degree at Oxford. A devout Puritan, Stoughton wisely left England when Charles II was restored to the throne, returning to Massachusetts where he gave up the ministry in favor of public life. As Chief Justice of the Court of Oyer and Terminer, he leaned heavily on Scriptures for guidance in determining the guilt or innocence of those brought before him. Like most of the younger ministers in Massachusetts, he was convinced that God restricted the devil's power to the extent that he could not impersonate by a spectre anyone other than an actual witch.

* * *

A spectral witch was one whose likeness was used by the devil to perform his work, even though the person whose likeness was being impersonated was some distance away and knew nothing of what was taking place. A covenant witch was one who had signed a pact, or covenant, with the devil, and willingly allowed his body and features to be used in whatever capacity the devil demanded.

* * *

During one period, there were more than 50 confessed witches in jail, none of whom was ever executed. Although these "confessors" were caught up in a number of lies, the Court took no action against them, the justices believing that they did not lie intentionally, but were made to do so by the devil. In spite of this, their testimony was used as evidence in a number of cases.

* * *

Although the "Body of Liberties" which was enacted by the General Court in 1641 prohibited the use of "barbarous and inhumane" torture to force a confession from a suspect, it did allow its use to learn the identity of any accomplices a convicted person might have had. This statute was broken a number of times during the witchcraft hysteria. Martha Carrier's two sons were accused of being witches, and confessed after they had been tied "neck and heels" until the blood poured out of their mouths. John Proctor's son was tied in a similar manner until he suffered a severe nosebleed, after which he was released by one of the more humane members of the group that was torturing him.

The torture that was the most difficult to withstand was the constant pleading of well-meaning relatives. Knowing that none of the confessors had been executed, they begged their loved ones to plead guilty to save their lives. A woman from Andover stated that her brother, who accompanied her to Salem when she was arrested, asked her to confess throughout the entire journey. Even after she was in jail, he and another man continued on in the same vein until she at last confessed that she was a witch.

The Andover Petition

We, whose names are underwritten, inhabitants of Andover, when as that horrible and tremendous judgment beginning at Salem-Village in the year 1692, (by some) call'd witchcraft, first breaking forth at Mr. Parris's house, several young persons being seemingly afflicted, did accuse several persons from afflicting them, and many there believing it to be so; we being informed that if a person were sick, that the afflicted persons could tell what or who was the cause of that sickness. Joseph Ballard of Andover (his wife being sick at the time) he either from himself, or by the advice of others, fetch'd two of the persons called the afflicted persons, from Salem Village to Andover. Which was the beginning of that dreadful calamity that befell us in Andover. And the authority in Andover, believing the said accusations to be true, sent for the said persons to come together to the meetinghouse in Andover (the afflicted persons being there). After Mr. Bernard had been at prayer, we were blindfolded and our hands were laid on the afflicted persons, they being in their fits, and falling into their fits at our coming into their presence (as they said), and some let us in and laid our hands upon them, and then they said they were well, and that we were guilty of afflicting them; whereupon we were all seized as prisoners, by a warrant from the Justice of the Peace, and forthwith carried to Salem. And by reason of that sudden surprisal, we knowing ourselves altogether innocent of that crime, we were all exceedingly astonished and amazed, and consternated and affrighted even out of our reason; and our nearest and dearest relations, seeing us in that dreadful condition, and knowing our great danger, apprehending that there was no othe way to save our lives as the case was then circumstanciated, but by our confessing ourselves to be such and such persons, as the afflicted represented us to be, they out of tender love and pity persuaded us to confess what we did confess. And indeed that confession, that is said we made, was no other than what was suggested to us by some gentlemen; they telling us that we were witches, and they knew it, and we knew it, and they knew we knew it, which made us think it were so; and our understanding, our reason, and our faculties almost gone, we were not capable of judging our condition; as also the hard measures they used with us, rendered us uncapable of making our defense; but said anything and everything which they desired, and most of what we said was a consenting of what they said. Sometime later, when we were better composed, they telling us what we had confessed, we did profess that we were innocent and ignorant of such things. And we hearing that Samuel Wardwell had renounced his confession, and quickly afterward condemned and executed, some of us were told we were going after Wardwell.
Mary Osgood, Mary Tiler, Deliverance Dane, Abigail Barker, Sarah Wilson, Hannah Tiler.

* * *

Under English Common Law, those persons convicted of witchcraft forfeited all their property to the government. After George Jacobs was arrested,

Sheriff Corwin and his deputies went to his farm where they impounded eight wagonloads of hay, all his livestock, 60 bushels of Indian corn, enough apples to make 24 barrels of cider, a gold thumb ring, a quantity of pewter, two brass kettles, and all the money, food, and furniture they could find.

They also tried to take his wife's ring from her finger, but she protested and struggled so vigorously that they finally allowed her to keep it. She begged them to leave her enough food for her evening meal, but they would do so only if she bought it from them. Since they had taken all her money, she was forced to beg food from her neighbors until the following May when her son returned home.

One of the strange aspects of this case was the fact that as the sheriff and his men were returning to Salem, they somehow managed to lose the two brass kettles which were never found.

* * *

Tituba remained in jail for approximately 15 months before she was finally freed. After the witchhunt was officially over, she revealed that "her Master (Parris) did beat her and otherwise abuse her, to make her confess and accuse (such as he called) her Sister-Witches, and that whatsoever she said . . . was the effect of such usage." This was denied by Parris who refused to pay her court and prison costs unless she retracted her accusation. Tituba stubbornly maintained that she had told the truth, and Parris just as stubbornly let her remain in jail until a wealthy Virginian purchased her by paying the province the money she owed.

* * *

SAMPLE OF WARRANT

"Warrant vs. Sarah Wildes and als.
Salem, April 21st 1692.
There being Complaint this day made (before us) by Thomas Putnam and John Buxton of Salem Village Yeoman in behalfe of theire Majes'ts for themselues and also for severall of theire neighbours Against William Hobs husbandman, Deliv'e his wife, Nehemiah Abot junior weaver, Mary Eastey, the wife of Isaac Eastey, and Sarah Wilds the wife of John Wilds, all of the town of Topsfield or Ipswich, and Edward Bishop husbandman and Sarah his wife of Salem Village, and Mary Black a negro of Leut. Nath. Putnam's of Salem Village also, and Mary English the wife of Phillip English merchant in Salem, for high suspition of sundry acts of witchcraft donne or Committed by them lately vpon the Body's of Anna putnam and Marcey Lewis belonging to the family of ye abouesd Thomas Putnam complaint and Mary Walcot ye daughter of Captain Jonathan Walcot of sd Salem Village and others, whereby great hurt and dammage hath benne donne to ye bodys of said persons abovenamed therefore craved Justice. You are therefore in their Majes'ts names

hereby required to Apprehend and bring before us William Hobs husbandman and his wife, Nehemiah Abot Junr Weaver, Mary Eastey the wife of Isaac Eastey, and all the abovenamed tomorrow about ten of the clock in the forenoon at the house of Lieut. Nath. Ingersolls in Salem Village in order to theire examination Relating to the premises abovesaid and hereof you are not to faile. Dated Salem, April 21st, 1692.

Jonathan Corwin John Hathorne Assists.

To George Herrick, Marshall of Essex, and any or all ye Constables in Salem or Topsfield or any other Towne."

* * *

The Death Warrant for Bridgette Bishop

To George Corwin, Gentleman High Sheriff of the County of Essex, Greeting:
Whereas Bridgett Bishop als Oliver the wife of Edward Bishop of Salem in the County of Essex Sawyer at a special Court of Oyer and Terminer Salem this second day of this instant month of June for the Countyes of Essex Middlesex and Suffolk where William Stoughton Esqr and his Associate Justices of the said Court was indicted and arraigned upon five severall indictments for using pracitising exorcising on the nyneteenth day of April last past and divers other dayes and times before and after certain acts of Witchcraft in and upon the bodies of Abigail Williams, Ann Putnam Junr Mercy Lewis, Mary Walcott and Elizabeth Hubbard of Salem Village singlewomen, whereby their bodies were hurt, afflicted pined, consumed Wasted and tormented contrary to the forme of the statute in the Case made and provided to which Indictmts the said Bridgette Bishop pleaded not guilty and for tryall thereof put her selfe upon God and her Country, whereupon she was found guilty of the Felonies and Witchcrafts whereof she stood Indicted and sentence of Death accordingly passed agt her as the law direct, Execution whereof yet remains to be done. These are therefore in the names of their Majesties William and Mary King and Queen over England and to will and command you That upon Friday next being the Tenth day of this instant month of June between the hours of eight and Twelve in the forenoon of the same day You safely conduct the sd Bridget Bishop als Oliver from their Majesties Gaol in Salem aforesaid to the place of Execution and there cause her to be hanged by the neck until she be dead and of your doings herein make return to the Clerk of the sd Court and precept and hereof you are not to fail at your peril And this shall be your sufficient Warrant Given under my hand & Seal at Boston the eighth day of June in the Fourth year of the Reigne of our Sovereigne Lord & William and Mary now King and Queen over England &c anno dom 1692.

Wm. Stoughton.

June 10th, 1692.

According to the within written precepts I have taken the body of the within named Bridget Bishop out of their Majesties Gaole in Salem and safely conveiged her to the place provided for her execution and caused the sd Bridgett to be hanged by the neck until She was dead (and buried in the place) all which was according to the time within Required and So I make Returne by me

George Corwin, Sheriff.

* * *

The "Body of Liberties," ratified by the Legislature in 1641, stated that two eyewitnesses to the same crime were needed to convict a suspect. This statute was ignored during the hysteria. Cotton Mather, who was convinced that witchcraft was a continuing crime, persuaded the Justices, at least two of whom were members of his congregation, that the testimony of an afflicted person plus that of someone who had witnessed the accused performing deeds that could only have been done with supernatural aid were enough to convict a suspect.

* * *

When the new Charter went into effect in 1692, the General Court passed a law stating that the province would continue all the laws pertaining to witchcraft that were not contrary to the laws of England. Although most of the clergy in Massachusetts felt that the Court should be guided by the Bible in the witchcraft cases, they failed to take into account the fact that although there are numerous references to witches and witchcraft in the Bible—the most notable of these being Exodus 22.18 which states, "Thou shalt not suffer a witch to live"—it does not define either of these terms.

* * *

Women had very few rights in colonial times. Despite this, the General Court passed a law on December 14, 1692 that allowed the widow of a condemned witch to keep her dowry and inheritance. This law also allowed a condemned witch to have the benefit of a Christian burial in hallowed ground, and also provided for milder punishments than the death penalty for lesser witchcraft-related crimes such as sorcery or divination. It was now possible for offenders to be punished by a short jail term, spending time in the pillory, or even by forced public confession. The offenders were also made to wear the names of their crimes in capital letters on their breasts for a period to be determined by the Court.

* * *

It has been suggested, and with good reason, that four ministers—Cotton Mather, Samuel Parris, Nicholas Noyes, and John Hale—were as committed to the fight against the forces of Satan as any other person in the province. A deposition signed by Sarah Ingersoll, the daughter of Nathaniel Ingersoll, stated that Sarah Churchill told her that she was sorry that she had confessed to signing the devil's book. Ingersoll told her that she was convinced that she had signed it, but Churchill insisted that she had not. Asked why she had confessed if she were innocent, Churchill said that "they" (Samuel Parris and Nicholas Noyes) threatened to throw her into a deep dungeon with George Burroughs and the other condemned witches if she refused. She claimed that if she told the ministers only one time that she had signed the book, they would believe her, but that if she denied having done so a hundred times, they would not.

* * *

In the cases of Susannah Martin, Elizabeth How, Martha Carrier, Sarah Good, and Bridget Bishop, much of the evidence against them concerned accidents and illnesses that affected the livestock of their neighbors. Although there are a number of plants in the New England area that might induce abnormal behavior and might even prove fatal to animals that eat them, the pioneers knew so little about them that they were inclined to attribute animal ailments, abnormal behavior, and deaths to witchcraft. Elizabeth How's brother-in-law was advised by one of his neighbors to use a form of sorcery to discover the identity of the person responsible for bewitching his cattle. Although the use of any form of sorcery was forbidden in Puritan Massachusetts, no action was taken against him for breaking the law.

* * *

The afflicted persons were able to see the spectres of the various witches who were banded together to destroy the Church of Christ in New England even though they were invisible to everyone else. Tituba and John Indian did not receive their spectral sight until after they had baked a cake of rye meal in which they had mixed the urine of Elizabeth Parris and Abigail Williams and fed the mixture to the Parris dog. This was suggested to them by Mary Sibley of Salem Village. Parris was so outraged by this use of sorcery in a Christian home that his sermon on the following Sunday was wholly directed to this subject, condemning John Indian, Tituba, and Mary Sibley by name.

* * *

The afflicted girls originally claimed that there were only 24 witches in Massachusetts, having learned this from seeing them assembled in the field behind the Salem Village parsonage. In time, the list surpassed the 400 mark, and might have gone even higher if the hysteria had been allowed to continue.

* * *

In July of 1692, the ghosts of French and Indian soldiers came out of the swamps to attack the colonial militia stationed in the garrison at Gloucester.

During the two weeks in which these attacks took place, the guns of the colonial militiamen very often misfired, while those that did shoot did no damage to the enemy.

On July 18, Major Samuel Appleton sent another sixty men to reinforce the Gloucester garrison. A small group of these soldiers was sent to find out what was causing a commotion about two miles from the garrison. When they neared their destination, they saw a man with bushy black hair and a blue shirt run out of the swamp and into the woods. Some of the men chased after him, but were unable to find him, and when they retraced their steps, they were also unable to find the stranger's footprints.

CONCLUSION

It is almost impossible to properly honor every one of the hundreds of brave men and women who courted exile and even death by daring to speak out against the madness. Rebecca Nurse, Martha Cory, John Proctor, and Constable John Willard were among those who lost their lives because of their outspoken beliefs, while a large number of others fled out of the province to escape the same fate.

Major Nathaniel Saltonstall, one of the original members of the Court of Oyer and Terminer, resigned his position after his colleagues sentenced Bridget Bishop to die, and when he returned to his home in Haverhill, he spoke out so strongly against the witchhunt that the afflicted persons cried out against him, some of them swearing that they had seen his spectre at several witch covens. The courageous man continued to speak out, and his attitude encouraged others to tak similar stands. A number of Boston Justices refused to serve on any witchcraft cases, stating that they would rather resign their commissions than be responsible for condemning good citizens on the type of evidence presented in the previous trials. Others soon follwed their lead, among them Simon Bradstreet, a former governor, and Thomas Danforth, a former Deputy Governor.

The most effective voices raised against the hysteria belonged to two Bostonians, Robert Calef and Thomas Brattle, who had been opposed to the witchhunt after attending Bridget Bishop's trial. They both attended many of the examinations and trials, interviewed a number of people who were familiar with the cases, and kept voluminous notes on what they learned. Brattle published his conclusions on October 8, 1692, in the form of a letter to a nonexistent minister. In it, he attacked the proceedings so incisively that this letter, distributed to all the members of the General Court and other influential men in the Colony, was one of the most important factors in bringing the witchcraft trials to an end.

Even after Governor Phips ordered the release of all the suspected witches who were then in jail, Cotton Mather refused to accept his ruling as final, and he continued to warn of the dangers the province still faced from the forces of Satan. Such was his fanaticism that he might have succeeded in having the hysteria erupt anew except for the material that Calef had patiently compiled. By 1697, his manuscript was completed, but the influence of the

Mather family was so great that no printer in New England would publish it, forcing Calef to take it to England where it was finally printed in 1700. Two years earlier, Cotton Mather wrote that "a sort of Sadduccee of this town hath written a Volume of invented and notorious lies" about the witchcraft cases and Mather's part in them, and when the book was distributed throughout the Colony, Increase Mather, then President of Harvard College, ostentatiously burned a copy of the "wicked book" which he banned throughout the school. In spite of their efforts, the Mathers were unable to suppress the book's sale, and its cold, hard logic helped the colonists to resist returning to a repetition of the hysteria of 1692.

THE WITCHCRAFT HYSTERIA OF 1692
Volume I   Leo Bonfanti

A carefully condensed history of the madness of 1692, with brief accounts of two other cases that preceded the more celebrated ones at Salem, and a study of the times that spawned this mass hysteria.

Volume II   Leo Bonfanti

This account of some of the more important stories of the witchcraft hysteria of 1692 includes those of John Proctor, George Burroughs, Susannah Martin, Dorcas Good, Mary Eastey, Martha Carrier, and others.

THE MASSACHUSETTS BAY COLONY
Volume I   Leo Bonfanti

A study of the Pilgrims to 1623, plus a brief history of the events that led to their emigration to America.

Volume II   Leo Bonfanti

The history of the Massachusetts Bay Colony from 1623, when the first settlement was made at Cape Ann, to 1644, the year that a second chamber, that of the Deputies, was added to the General Court.

EXCERPTS FROM THE BOSTON COOK BOOK OF 1883

A selection of recipes that were being used in New England in the 17th, 18th, and 19th centuries.

FAVORITE ITALIAN RECIPES
                                                                            Leo Bonfanti

Some of the Italian recipes that helped to change the culinary habits of New Englanders.

SUMMARY OF THE WITCHCRAFT HYSTERIA OF 1692
                                                                            Leo Bonfanti

An easily understood summary of the witchcraft hysteria of 1692.